Youth
Problems
and
Law
Enforcement

Prentice-Hall
Essentials of Law Enforcement Series

James D. Stinchcomb
Series Editor

Youth
Problems
and
Law
Enforcement

EDWARD ELDEFONSO

Supervisor, Santa Clara County
Juvenile Probation Department,
San Jose, California

De Anza College

West Valley College

PRENTICE-HALL, INC.
Englewood Cliffs, New Jersey

ISBN: P-0-13-982306-9
        C-0-13-982314-X
Library of Congress Card Catalog Number: 77-171351
Printed in the United States of America

10 9 8 7 6 5 4 3 2 1

PRENTICE-HALL INTERNATIONAL, INC., *London*
PRENTICE-HALL OF AUSTRALIA PTY. LTD., *Sydney*
PRENTICE-HALL OF CANADA LTD., *Toronto*
PRENTICE-HALL OF INDIA PRIVATE LIMITED, *New Delhi*
PRENTICE-HALL OF JAPAN, INC., *Tokyo*

Introduction

Surely nothing can be more fundamental to guaranteeing the delivery of professional services than the employment of properly trained personnel. In pursuit of that goal, law enforcement officers and those who train them have long recognized the need for concise yet thoroughly documented information, well-researched and accurately presented.

In recent years, several commendable efforts have resulted in the availability of some valuable training resources. But too few of these were professionally developed by the textbook publishing companies, although their assistance was becoming imperative. The Prentice-Hall Essentials of Law Enforcement Series has been developed following a conference of national authorities who were asked to determine topics for priority production. The subject areas chosen are both timely and critical to the police and to their own increased determination to improve their service.

The potential use for this series is limited only by the creative imaginations of those responsible for peace officers' access to learning. Each book may perform as a supplement to a college course, as a resource for a training program, or as a reader to encourage informal study. It is the hope and the intent of the publisher, the editor, and the authors that these practical texts will contribute to the continuing progress being achieved by the nation's police.

James D. Stinchcomb

Virginia Commonwealth University

Preface

Modern Western society has evolved the police as a specialized social agency to preserve peace, to enforce laws, and to protect life and property. In recent years, however, the traditional police role has broadened to include many aspects of social service formerly the exclusive domain of other social institutions such as churches, schools, and public welfare departments. The police today are involved in prevention, identification, and early reversal of aberrant social processes. They, like every other agency of society, are vitally concerned with problems such as the costly cycle of school dropouts, unemployment, and welfare dependency, as well as crime and delinquency.

Basic police responsibility with both juveniles and adults is placed on the policeman on the beat, whether on foot or in a motor vehicle. He is responsible for maintaining law and order on his beat, with specialized personnel including the *juvenile unit* available to assist him in larger departments. The patrolman is in no way relieved of his basic responsibility and authority for police-juvenile relations by the availability of a juvenile unit; he remains the key person for deterring and controlling antisocial acts affecting all citizens, including minors. And, in fact, statistics compiled by the FBI and the Department of Health, Education and Welfare (Children's Bureau) reveal that juveniles are more often initially contacted by patrolmen performing general police functions than they are by juvenile specialists. Thus, in terms of both job responsibilities and job realities, the patrolman *must* be aware of the principles and approved practices relating to police work with juveniles.

The purpose of this book is to provide a resource in training prospective police officers as well as practitioners in the complexity of youth problems. The book's philosophy is therefore quite simple: to introduce the subject of juvenile delinquency in a manner that serves the needs of law enforcement personnel. It is based on a variety of personal experiences, including the teaching of police science classes in Juvenile Procedures, Police-Community Relations, the writing of several textbooks in law enforcement, and 15 years of field experience in the area of juvenile delinquency.

This book approaches the problem of juvenile delinquency from the viewpoint that police are primarily responsible for enforcing law and only indirectly responsible for the resolution of social problems. But in recognition of the expanded role of the police and out of respect for the courage and dignity with which the police have confronted the enormous tasks related to juvenile delinquency in this era, the book seeks to isolate the nature and scope of delinquency and its impact on law enforcement.

The complexity of crime and delinquency virtually preclude a definitive treatment. In fact, a single volume could scarcely *survey* the literature available on the problem. Still, I have tried to clarify some of the confusing aspects of the youthful offender that relate to the police and, at the same time, present an overview of the entire problem of juvenile delinquency. With this approach, I hope to go beyond mere presentation of subject matter toward the more rewarding goal of stimulating both understanding of the problem and pride in law enforcement careers.

Acknowledgements

It is impossible to give due acknowledgement for all of the assistance I have had in preparing *Youth Problems and Law Enforcement*. Much of it has come through the years, from day-to-day contacts with teachers, probation officers, police officers, lawyers, criminologists, and many others. However, I must give special acknowledgement to several individuals. Grateful acknowledgement is due my wife, Mildred, whose amicable disposition made completion of this project less difficult; B. Earl Lewis, Director, Department of Law Enforcement Education, DeAnza College, who was responsible for my *first* venture in the field of education several years ago; Alan Coffey, Training Officer, Santa Clara County Juvenile Probation Department and coauthor in other projects, including *Principles of Law Enforcement, Human Relations: Law Enforcement in a Changing Community, Police-Community Relations, An Introduction to Corrections: A Part of the Criminal Justice System*, and *Criminal Law and the Policeman*. My gratitude is further expressed to the afore-mentioned colleague and friend for permitting me to draw upon information from his paper, "Theories of Deviant Behavior." And, finally, I express my thanks to those in-dividuals who administer the most progressive juvenile re-habilitation program in the State of California: Robert E. Nino, Chief Juvenile Probation Officer, Santa Clara County, San Jose, California, and his assistants: Richard Bothman, Michael Kuzirian, David Lagassé, Pedro Silva, and Eunice C. Peterson.

Edward Eldefonso

Contents

Youth
Problems
and
Law
Enforcement

Perspective of Delinquency: Definition

Delinquent behavior in the United States is costly not only in terms of dollars and cents, but also in terms of priceless human resources. The cost of delinquent acts and the related expenses of law enforcement, the administration of justice, and the maintenance of juvenile correctional institutions are relatively easy to compute. But the costs of delinquency's emotional interference with our organized ways of living and its harmful effects on both victims and offenders are virtually impossible to calculate. It is important to note that juvenile delinquency is related to criminal behavior and that patterns of antisocial youthful behavior are often carried over into adult activities. Many acts which are called delinquent when engaged in by juveniles would be considered criminal if committed by adults.

The extent of juvenile delinquency in our country cannot be determined exactly, although the evidence indicates that delinquent behavior known to official agencies has increased in recent years, both absolutely and proportionately. This area—the size of the problem—will be discussed in Chapter 2. At this point, our main objective is to try to define the blanket term, "juvenile delinquency," which obscures rather than clarifies our understanding of youthful misbehavior. What is delinquency? Who are the delinquents? How do they differ from nondelinquents?

Juvenile delinquency describes the antisocial behavior of many different types of youth who are in trouble or on the verge of trouble with the law. The delinquent may range from the normal, mischievous youngsters, or the youth who is involved in delinquent activities by accident, to the youth who knowingly and purposefully commits offenses. In general

chapter

1

usage, "juvenile delinquency" is a catch-all term; it means different things to different people. For example, to some, the manner of attire—the mere wearing of a mod outfit or long hair—is sufficient to label a child a delinquent. To a homeowner who strives hard to keep his lawn looking neat, a delinquent may be a youth who rides a bicycle across his lawn. To one who reads the lurid newspaper headlines about teen-agers, a delinquent conjures up a picture of a youth hoodlum who robs, steals, and murders. These are three popular misconceptions of juvenile delinquents, and they obviously vary widely.

As the following analysis will indicate, the question "What is delinquency?" may itself be highly misleading because it suggests that a single answer is possible. In view of the variety of *legal, administrative, clinical,* and *behavioral* definitions available, the assumption that any directly factual, mutually consistent answer is possible may itself be one of the principal sources of confusion about delinquency. Consequently, one of the first requirements of discussion is to reject the simple question "What is delinquency?" and to substitute the question "What is meant when the term *delinquency* is used?"

The Legal Definition

Legally speaking, a juvenile delinquent is a minor who commits a delinquent act as defined by law and who is adjudicated as such by an appropriate court. But even laws which many think of as being absolute or definitive are not so regarding juvenile delinquency. Most juvenile court laws define as a delinquent a juvenile who violates any state or local law or commits any act that would be considered a crime if committed by an adult. In addition, however, most statutes define as delinquency acts which are violations of laws only when committed by children: truancy, running away, incorrigibility, and ungovernable behavior. In the latter categories, the law ceases to be definitive and becomes varied and subjective.

A distinction is usually made between *delinquency* and *pre-delinquency* in terms of relative danger posed to the community, as well as in terms of whether certain offenses are law violations for children only. In general, delinquency refers to acts which pose a greater danger to the community and which carry formal sanctions for either adult or juvenile. Pre-delinquency, on the other hand, generally refers to an offense carrying legal sanctions only for children. Pre-delinquency may or may not lead to "actual delinquency" but is nevertheless here defined as *deviance*—deviance meaning deviation from a societal norm of some kind or another. Of course, this definition of deviance would encompass mental illness also. Deviance refers to the deviation from norms legally defined as requiring action by either the juvenile court or the juvenile court staff.

The law's vagueness in defining delinquency can only lead to questioning. When is a child normally rebellious and when is he an incorrigible delinquent? When is he just socializing with the neighborhood children and when is he loitering? And why is smoking delinquent today and perfectly acceptable a week from today when a youth reaches his eighteenth birthday? Also, why should a child who impulsively runs away because of a minor dispute with his parents share the appellation, delinquent, with the youngster who robs a filling station?

As a *legal concept*, delinquency is considerably broader and vaguer than the legal concept of crime—for two reasons: (1) It includes many behaviors that would not be considered illegal if committed by adults; and (2) A description of these behaviors is frequently much more ambiguous than would be constitutionally acceptable in criminal statutes, which generally require precise specifications of the activities labeled as illegal. The New Jersey and California juvenile delinquency statutes provide a representative modern example:

> Juvenile delinquency (in the aforementioned states) is hereby defined as the commission by a child under 18 years of age (under 21 years in the State of California) of:
>
> 1) Any act which when committed by a person of the age of 18 (21 in the State of California) or over would constitute:
>   a. A felony, high misdemeanor, a misdemeanor or other offense, or

The Legal Definition

b. The violation of any penal law or municipal ordinance, or

c. An act or offense for which he could be prosecuted in the method partaken of the nature of a criminal action or proceeding, or

d. Being a disorderly person, or

2) The following acts:

e. Habitual vagrancy, or

f. Incorrigibility, or

g. Immorality, or

h. Knowingly associating with thieves or vicious or immoral persons, or

i. Growing up in idleness or delinquency, or

j. Knowingly visiting gambling places or patronizing other places of establishments, his (or her) admission to which constitutes a violation of law, or

k. Idly roaming the streets at night, or

l. Habitual truancy from school, or

m. Deportment endangering the morals, health or general welfare of said child.[1]

Although the New Jersey and California juvenile court laws apparently do not differ significantly, there is no doubt that such closely related laws are unusual. Laws vary among different states. Just who is considered to be a child is different in different states. So are the types of misbehavior included under the broad term of delinquency. Thus, it is quite possible for a child to be considered a delinquent in one state and not one in another. But the most cursory review of this "typical" inventory of delinquent behavior should make two conclusions abundantly clear: (1) Many of the activities specified as delinquent are no different from those engaged in, at one time or another, by all children; (2) Since either all or the vast majority of children at one time or another engage in these activities, and since only a small proportion of these children are either socially labeled or officially processed as delinquents, *something more than the mere engagement in these activities is required for the social identification of a child as a delinquent.* This "something more" is formal, administrative action on the part of the law enforcement agents of society.[2]

[1] R. R. Korn, "The Counseling of Delinquents," *Training Aid No. 1,* Santa Clara County Juvenile Probation Department, San Jose, Calif., 1968, p. 3 (mimeographed).

[2] *Ibid.* p. 4.

Perspective of Delinquency: Definition

Administrative Definitions
of Delinquency

Formal administrative action by law enforcement agents, according to Dr. Richard Korn, may take several forms, and estimates of the extent of delinquency will vary according to the index used.[3] If *police complaints* are used, one figure will result; if *court appearances* are used, the figure will be different; if *commitments to an institution* are used, a third figure will result. In a study investigating the estimates of delinquency made on the basis of these different indices of delinquency, it was noted that the formal law enforcement action often went beyond "recorded police complaints." One group of children were *not* taken to court and were not formally adjudicated delinquent—and they were not institutionalized—though there is no reason to believe that their misbehavior was significantly less serious than the behavior of the adjudicated and institutionalized children. Therefore, it can be said that the only differentiation between the non-adjudicated and non-institutionalized delinquents from the others was not in what they did but in the manner in which their cases were handled by agents of the society. Needless to say, if *police complaints* are utilized as an index of delinquency (in contrast to court appearances or commitments to institutions), the rate of delinquency will show a drastic increase in any particular area. In other words, it is common knowledge that almost without exception the police officer is the first to approach a child in trouble. It is also common knowledge that many youngsters are handled on an unofficial basis and not referred to a juvenile court. Thus, the police officer, in effect, sits as judge or serves as social worker in many instances. He may also determine the final disposition of about half of the cases involving juvenile offenders who are taken into custody.[4]

[3]*Ibid.*, p. 40.
[4]*Juvenile Court Statistical Series*, United States Dept. of Health, Education and Welfare, Children's Bureau, U. S. Government Printing Office, Washington, D. C., 1969.

Delinquents and Nondelinquents:
How Do They Differ?

Individuals *not familiar* with the problem of juvenile delinquency would readily agree that there is no similarity between a delinquent and a nondelinquent. However, studies by George Vold and Austin L. Porterfield show that there is no significant difference between the delinquent and the nondelinquent populations.[5] Furthermore, according to *Korn*:

> There is no valid basis for assuming that the behavior of officially adjudicated delinquents differs significantly from the illegal behavior of a vastly larger population of children, committing similar acts, who are not formally processed as delinquents. What strikingly differentiates the officially processed delinquents from those whose behavior is either not detected, or not officially acted upon, is a chain of social-like processes ranging from the (a) arrests, (b) formal adjudication as delinquent, (c) official supervision and restriction within the open community to (d) brief or prolonged incarceration in the enforced company of similarly processed children in correctional institutions. . . .

> . . . the most visible and demonstrable difference derives not from the nature of the delinquent behavior itself, but rather from the nature and extent of the community reactions to this behavior—reactions ranging from tolerance to indifference, or indifference to prolonged correctional incarceration. We have, in effect, implied that it makes a difference whether or not juvenile misbehavior is tolerated and ignored ("Don't worry, he'll grow out of it"), informally dealt with in the family setting ("He'll get what's coming to him when Dad comes home"), or formally punished by the impersonal law enforcement agents of society ("We hereby commit you during the period of your minority to the New York State Training School at Otisville").[6]

The problem of defining delinquency is further compounded when the various agencies that deal with delinquency tend to develop their own concepts of delinquent conduct. Agencies such as police, school, and the juvenile

[5]G. Vold and A. L. Porterfield, *Youth in Trouble* (Austin, Texas: The Leo Potishman Foundation, 1946).

[6]R. R. Korn, "The Counseling of Delinquents," *Training Aid No. 1*, p. 6.

court have devised their own concepts of juvenile delinquents. These "other concepts" are discussed in the following.[7]

Police Concept

The police concept classifies the delinquent as the *statistical delinquent* or the *personality-disordered delinquent*. The statistical delinquent is the youngster who is involved in a delinquent act through impulsiveness or immaturity. For example, he may be involved in an automobile theft without, at that time, realizing the consequences of his actions. Such actions usually occur on the spur of the moment while the youngster is engaged with other children. However, this youngster is not recidivistic and responds to agency services provided. Nevertheless, he is a "statistic" and this impulsive delinquent act is reported by the arresting agency and, in some cases, in a subsequent referral to the juvenile court.

On the other hand, the *personality-disordered delinquent* is the youth who is often involved in antisocial acts. In most instances, his behavior eventually necessitates a referral to the juvenile court and, usually, custodial care or some type of official help. The personality-disordered delinquent is the youngster who often runs the gamut of agency referrals. In other words, he may have received numerous warnings by law enforcement agencies prior to referral to the juvenile court. Furthermore, after being processed by the juvenile court, he may be placed back in the custody of his parents on probation on several occasions. However, agency services have failed, and institutionalization is often the end result.

School Concept

The school concept is a rather general one. It appears that schools, or the educational system, are concerned with delinquents who fall into several categories, such as:

1. The academic delinquent—a minor who is not working to full capacity in school.
2. The behavioral delinquent—a boy or girl who is unable to respond to demands made upon him by his teachers or is continually involved in altercations with his peers.

[7]E. Eldefonso, *Law Enforcement and the Youthful Offender: Juvenile Procedures* (New York: John Wiley and Sons, Inc., 1967), pp. 11–12.

3. The mentally or physically retarded delinquent—a child who is unable to compete with his classmates due to severe emotional or physical handicaps, thereby causing him to act out in a hostile, unacceptable manner.

Generally, the school is of the opinion that an unhappy child is a potential delinquent. As an example, the school cites the case of the youngster who is unable to keep up with the manner of dress utilized by his peers or the youngster who will not conform to dress standards. This youngster may be teased and taunted by his peers. Eventually, he is provoked into striking back. Is this a delinquent? No, but the seed is planted.

Juvenile Court Concept

The juvenile court concept deals with the juvenile who is actually referred to the juvenile probation department by one of various agencies. The probation officer may file a petition on the youth's behalf, alleging a *law violation*. Of course, not all minors who appear before the court appear on a delinquency petition. As previously discussed, numerous youngsters appear before the juvenile court in pre-delinquent behavior and dependency situations. Only the youngster petitioned for a penal code law violation should be classified as a delinquent.

Thus, according to the juvenile court concept, no juvenile is a delinquent unless he appears before the court on a petition alleging a law violation and the court sustains said petition. The juvenile court contends that it would be unjust to declare a juvenile a delinquent at the point of his apprehension. The adult is presumed to be innocent until proven guilty. According to the juvenile court concept, the juvenile should be accorded the same presumption.

As stated earlier, about 50 percent of the juveniles apprehended after violating the law are released by police without official action and very few are referred to the court. Thus, there is a legal difference between the youngster's being apprehended as a juvenile delinquent and being found to be a delinquent in a juvenile court proceeding. The juvenile court concept suggests that a minor does have due process and that his legal rights are protected. From the legal point of view, until such time as a court of a competent jurisdiction passes upon the evidence and makes a finding that the juvenile is a delinquent, the child is no more delinquent than the adult who is not a criminal until he is properly charged with an offense against the law and is found guilty as charged.

Dependent, Neglected, and Abused Children

Authorities in the field of probation, parole, and corrections acknowledge the fact that much of our delinquency problem derives from dependent, neglected, and abused children. Research on delinquency reveals that many of the youngsters involved in law violations were, at one time, processed through the juvenile court as dependent, neglected, or abused children. Even when such cases were not handled officially by the juvenile court, police files indicate that "unofficial" contacts (i.e., field contacts handled without official referral to the juvenile court) had occurred.

Therefore, it is incumbent upon the law enforcement officer to have some knowledge of these "pre-delinquent" youngsters.

Who Are They?

Two small children quarrel fretfully in a filthy room, while their brother lies wet and listless on a bare, stained mattress. Their older sister comes in carrying a small bag of potato chips and, for a few moments, there is the noise of children arguing over food. Their mother will not be home until the early hours of the morning. When she comes, she is likely to be drunk. Their father is a stranger to them. They live a cold, lonely, uncertain existence (Figure 1–1).

In another neighborhood, a three-year-old boy lies unconscious in the arms of his mother at the emergency hospital. Beside them sits her boyfriend, 22 years old. The couple share a small apartment, they reluctantly tell the attending physician. The "accident" occurred at their apartment. The boy had picked up a cigar and eaten it; approximately an

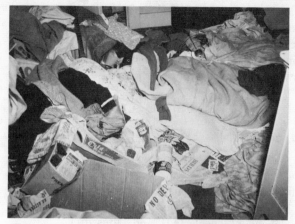

Fig. 1–1a

Fig. 1–1b

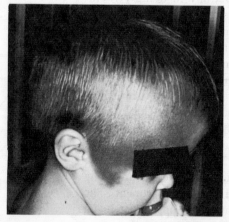

Fig. 1.2. Courtesy of Michael McDonald, Santa Clara County Juvenile Probation Department, San Jose, California.

Perspective of Delinquency: Definition

hour later, according to the couple, the child started to gag and was having difficulty breathing. With this explanation, they hand the child to the doctor, requesting assistance. But the child is beyond all human help. He dies soon after admission to the hospital.

The autopsy discloses no evidence of tobacco. It does reveal, however, a fractured skull, elbow abrasions, bruises, and multiple internal injuries (Figure 1–2).

Confronted with this evidence, the boyfriend admits he had beaten the boy. He is subsequently indicted for murder.

Since the assistant district attorney can not prove murder (the child had been severely beaten by his mother prior to her boyfriend's fatal blows), the charge is reduced to involuntary manslaughter and the young mother's boyfriend is committed to state prison for six months to ten years.

Child neglect and *abuse* are not new phenomena in our society, or in any society. What is new is the increase and violence in the attacks on infants and young children by parents, guardians, or other custodians. Dependency and neglect are similar. A neglected child appears before the court and is adjudged a *dependent child of the court.*

Are these children fictional characters or mere statistical rarities? By no means. They are the children of neglect and abuse whom we seldom notice among the bulk of happy children. Sometimes neighbors, relatives, or school personnel will be aware that something is wrong, but frequently no one is concerned until a crisis or death brings the situation to public knowledge.

The line between neglect and abuse is sometimes difficult to draw, but the two can generally be distinguished by determining the degree of intention present. The *neglectful parent usually does not consciously intend to harm his child,* but through failure to meet the child's health, nutritional, comfort, and emotional needs, he exposes the child to severe risks. Testimony before a Committee on Social Welfare gave some examples of neglect, such as the father who left his four small children alone in a car with a book of matches. Although nothing happened to them, he was charged with neglect. One

[8]*Protective Services for Children*, Report of the Assembly Interim Committee on Social Welfare, Published by The Assembly of the State of California, January 1967, pp. 6–10.

Dependent, Neglected, and Abused Children

month later, he left two of the children alone in the car. One, a small girl, lit some matches and subsequently died of burns. Many parents may leave children alone at a time of emergency or under unusual circumstances, but it is those parents who habitually leave their children alone who expose them to the greatest risks.

Living requires some exposure to risks. The more serious the risk, and the longer and more repeatedly the child is exposed to it, the greater is the neglect. For example, an occasional missed meal is no great cause for concern, but continual failure to feed children results in malnutrition or starvation.

Besides failure to feed children, neglect includes leaving children alone, maintaining them in unsanitary conditions, keeping them out of school, failing to keep them clean and adequately dressed, and ignoring their medical needs. As in the case of feeding, concrete circumstances and conditions determine the existence and extent of neglect. A parent who leaves his children in a parked car for a few moments while he runs in to buy a package of cigarettes would not be considered neglectful according to prevailing community standards. But a parent who leaves his children in the car all day, particularly if they are very young and the sun is hot or there is a great deal of traffic, is probably neglectful, since the likelihood of harm over the long run is very substantial. A parent who sends his six-year-old child out to play during the day is not neglectful, but if he locks his three-year-old out at night, especially in winter, he is being neglectful.

Most neglectful families show neglect in a variety of ways. A young Sacramento mother, whose husband was imprisoned on a narcotics violation, was overwhelmed with the care of five little boys, the oldest of whom was five. She sat watching television all day long while the boys defecated, vomited, and urinated in the house, tracked mud in with their bare feet, and fed themselves uncooked maggoty oats from a bag in the kitchen cupboard. When a complaint brought a probation officer to the scene, she found the boys filthy, emaciated, and covered with sores, the house overrun with insects and vermin, and an unbearable stench permeating the atmosphere. On the basis of the combination of circumstances, the situation was classified as one of general neglect. It was the extreme conditions in the home, the evidence of

Perspective of Delinquency: Definition

the duration of these conditions for a considerable period of time, and the very youthful age of the children that defined the circumstances as neglect.

Abuse Varies

In contrast to the neglectful parent, the abusive parent intends to harm his child and does so by overt action. Sexual assault, mutilation, and tying up in a dark closet are examples of abuse.

The literature on abuse shows that children may be beaten with ironing cords, sticks, wires, or lead pipes. They may be tortured with lighted cigarettes, scalding water, or hot stoves (Figure 1–3). Beloved pets may be tormented

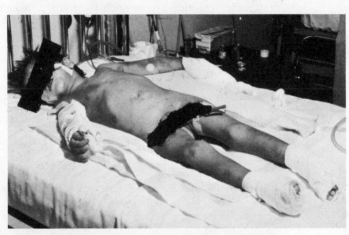

Fig. 1.3a
Courtesy of Michael McDonald, Santa Clara County Juvenile Probation Department, San Jose, California.

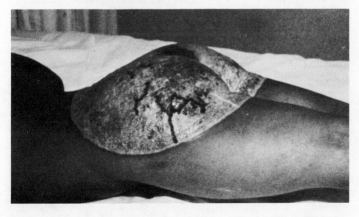

Fig. 1.3b
Courtesy of Michael McDonald, Santa Clara County Juvenile Probation Department, San Jose, California.

Dependent, Neglected, and Abused Children

and killed before their eyes and the children threatened with the same fate. Parents have twisted their offsprings' arms and legs until they broke, slammed them against the wall until their skulls were fractured, and even bitten them.

Ninety percent of these abusive parents show no remorse. They blame their children for being "monsters," "idiots," or "crazy." Often one child is singled out as a scapegoat. One abusive father shaved his son's head and referred to him as "the criminal." Other parents give seemingly irrelevant reasons for attacking their children: "He broke a milk bottle" might be offered as an excuse for knocking a youngster to the floor.

The intensity of the activity helps define it as abuse. A parent may habitually spank a child without this constituting abuse, as long as injury does not result. Of course, the child may suffer emotionally in such a situation, which brings us to another category, not currently covered in the law, the category of emotional abuse or neglect.

Statistical Information on Dependent and Neglected Children

Most juvenile courts have jurisdiction over court actions involving dependent and neglected children, as well as delinquent children. As revealed in Tables 1–1, 1–2, and 1–3,

Table 1–1

Number and Rate of Dependency and Neglect Cases Disposed of by Juvenile Courts, United States, 1969[a]

Type of Court	Number of Cases	Rate per 1,000 Child Population[b]			
		All Courts	Age Jurisdiction of Court		
			Under 16	Under 17	Under 18[c]
Urban	83,800	2.5	1.8	3.3	2.5
Semi-urban	31,500	3.0	1.6	3.3	3.3
Rural	11;700	1.4	1.0	1.6	1.4

[a]Based on the data from 1,636 courts whose jurisdiction includes almost three-fourths of the child population under 18 years of age.
[b]Calculated on basis of the 1960 child population at risk, that is, the child population under 16, for courts whose age jurisdiction is under 16, etc.
[c]A small number of courts having jurisdiction of children under 21 years of age are included here. The number of cases involved do not seriously affect the rates of the courts in this column.
Source: U. S. Department of Health, Education and Welfare, Children's Bureau (Washington D. C.: U. S. Government Printing Office, 1969), p. 10.

Table 1–2

Percent Change in Dependency and Neglect Cases Disposed of by Juvenile Courts, United States, 1969[a]

Type of Court	Total	Judicial	Nonjudicial
Total	−10	−3	−28
Urban	−10	−5	−28
Semi-urban	−10	+3	−35
Rural	−10	−9	−17

[a]Based on data from 1,506 courts reporting both years, whose jurisdiction includes over two-thirds of the child population under 18 years of age.
Source: U. S. Department of Health, Education and Welfare, Children's Bureau (Washington, D. C.: U. S. Government Printing Office, 1969), p. 11.

dependency and neglect cases (including those physically abused) in the United States totaled 127,000 in 1969, a decline of nearly 10 percent from the 1968 figure. This continues the decline *first noted* in 1967 in the number of dependency and neglect cases being handled by the juvenile courts.

Summary

This chapter introduces the student to the problem of *legally* identifying a delinquent. What is delinquency? Who are the delinquents? How do they *differ* from nondelinquents? These questions are asked and, as the chapter progresses, answered.

Legally, a juvenile delinquent is one who commits any act that if committed by an adult would constitute a crime. Other "pre-delinquent" types of misbehavior (i.e., ungovernable behavior, incorrigibility, or habitual disobedience beyond the lawful control of parent or other lawful authority) are relegated to a separate category.

In describing the difficulties encountered in defining delinquency, the chapter also examines other definitions of delinquency, such as the police, school, and juvenile court concepts. These concepts are treated in a section dealing with the "difference" between delinquents and nondelinquents. Indications are that there is no significant difference between

Summary

Table 1–3
Number and Rate of Dependency and Neglect Cases Disposed of by Juvenile Courts, United States, 1946–1969[a]

Year	Number of Cases	Rate[b]
1946	101,000	2.4
1947	104,000	2.4
1948	103,000	2.3
1949	98,000	2.1
1950	93,000	1.9
1951	97,000	2.1
1952	98,000	1.9
1953	103,000	1.9
1954	103,000	1.9
1955	106,000	1.9
1956	105,000	1.8
1957	114,000	1.9
1958	124,000	2.0
1959	128,000	2.0
1960	131,000	2.0
1961	140,000	2.1
1962	141,000	2.0
1963	146,000	2.1
1964	150,000	2.1
1965	157,000	2.2
1966	161,000	2.2
1967	154,000	2.1
1968	141,000	1.9
1969	127,000	1.7

[a]Data for 1955–1969 estimated from courts serving about two-thirds of the child population under 18 years of age in the United States. Data prior to 1955 estimated by the Children's Bureau, based on reports from a smaller but comparable group of courts. Inclusion of estimates from Alaska and Hawaii beginning in 1960 does not materially affect trend.
[b]Based on dependency and neglect cases per 1,000 U. S. child population under 18 years of age.
Source: U. S. Department of Health, Education and Welfare, Children's Bureau (Washington, D. C.: U. S. Government Printing Office, 1969), p. 12.

the delinquent and nondelinquent populations. Reasons for arriving at this conclusion are discussed. In essence, it is concluded that the most visible and demonstrable difference derives not from the type of act committed, but rather from the reaction or lack of reaction to youthful offenders by the community.

Perspective of Delinquency: Definition

The chapter concludes with a brief discussion of dependent, neglected, and abused children. The differences between each category—dependency, neglect, and abuse—are identified.

Selected References

BLOCH, H. A., and G. GEIS, *Man, Crime and Society*, Chap. 3. New York: Random House, Inc., 1962.

CAVAN, R. S., *Juvenile Delinquency*, pp. 16–17. Philadelphia: Lippincott, 1962.

ELDEFONSO, E., *Law Enforcement and the Youthful Offender: Juvenile Procedures*, Chap. 2. New York: John Wiley & Sons, Inc., 1967.

MARTIN, M. M., and J. P. FITZPATRICK, *Delinquent Behavior: A Redefinition of the Problem*, Chap. 1. New York: Random House, Inc., 1965.

TAPPAN, P. W., *Juvenile Delinquency*, Appendix B. New York: McGraw-Hill Book Company, 1949.

Scope
and
Nature
of
the
Problem:
Measurement
and
Statistics

✗ Each year about two million youngsters commit *known* acts of juvenile delinquency. Approximately three-fourths of these cases are handled directly by the police and family, and the rest are taken to court. The problem of delinquency is a serious one; though it is estimated that not more than 5 percent of all youths get into trouble, the number of arrests of youths under 18 has doubled in the last ten years.[1] In auto thefts alone, according to statistical information compiled by the Federal Bureau of Investigation and the Children's Bureau, youthful offenders account for 64 percent of all arrests.[2] They represent 52 percent of arrests for burglary, 49 percent for larceny, and 26 percent for robbery.[3] It would seem, also, that in poor, densely populated slum neighborhoods of larger cities, the juvenile delinquency rate is very rapidly getting out of hand. The statistical information from

[1] *Juvenile Court Statistical Series*, U. S. Department of Health, Education and Welfare (Washington, D. C.: U. S. Government Printing Office, 1969).
[2] Uniform Crime Reports, Federal Bureau of Investigation (Washington D. C.: U. S. Government Printing Office, 1970).
[3] *Ibid.*

chapter
2

the aforementioned agencies reveals that in slum neighborhoods the juvenile delinquency rate is three times as great as in other areas. This is not to say, however, that the delinquency trend in rural areas has not increased tremendously— a 16 percent increase in rural delinquency occurred in 1969.

Limitations on the Measurement of Crime and Delinquency

Although juvenile delinquency is clearly a major problem in our society, it is impossible to determine just how significant recent increases in the problem may be. In order to evaluate these increases, we are forced to rely on statistics. While statistics show that there are certainly more crimes committed by juveniles in proportion to the increasing population than heretofore, they are available for only the past 15 to 20 years. Statistical evaluation of juvenile delinquency is thus relatively new, and there is not enough evidence to say with certainty that the overall problem is actually increasing.

It is also probable that two other factors have strongly influenced the upward trend of recent years. The first factor, which has been mentioned before, is the fact that the police are apprehending more juveniles, just as they are taking into custody more adults. As adult crime increases, juvenile crime also tends to rise. The second factor, which is most important in interpreting crime statistics, is that the police are arresting people today for behavior that was not even considered criminal in previous years. Two actual cases serve as examples:

> Me, I get a bad deal at home. My old man is always riding me about getting out and going to work and getting more money to help out. My mother, well, she was alright I guess. She kept after me too about my grades in school. So I just took off. I was going to go to Florida or some place like that and join the Army. Even if I am only 17, I figure I could get in. Well, I started hitchin' and I got some rides, and I was about 200 miles away from my home when I was picked up. It seems like every cop in the country was out after me and everybody was treating me like I had done something terrible.

Limitations on the Measurement of Crime and Delinquency

> This boy and I were going around for about three years. We talked about marriage and our folks laughed at first, and then they got sore about it. He was called into the Army, and the night before he left we got carried away and made love. Well, I had a baby. My parents treated me like I was a criminal or had done something dirty. Then, my boyfriend got picked up and jailed on statutory rape. I was 16 and he was 19.

Cases of this type are frequently seen in any police station. The first case involves a boy, age 17, who leaves home to join the Army. We call him a runaway, a juvenile problem. The second case, that of the unwed mother, presents a similar situation. At an earlier time, neither case would have been classified as delinquency. Thus, we find that changing cultural attitudes and conditions often present difficulties in recording and interpreting crime statistics.

According to R. H. Beattie, a noted authority on criminal statistics, one of the first realizations necessary in the field of statistical crime reporting is the fact that crime is not just one kind of antisocial behavior, but a complex of many kinds and types of human behavior.[4] Crime, therefore, is not a homogeneous phenomenon and cannot be measured with a single yardstick. The tendency for one type of criminal or delinquent behavior to increase or decrease may have no relationship whatever to other types of criminal or delinquent behavior that are also changing in volume.

> The first requirement generally stated for a system of criminal statistics is to know the amount and extent of crime, and the number and kinds of criminals. Crimes can be accounted for only through those special agencies set up to enforce criminal law. Thus has come the general axiom that crimes can be counted best in terms of the known offenses reported to police agencies. Obviously, no one will ever know actually how many criminal offenses are committed. The number and extent of unknown offenses may be a subject of speculation, but not of measurement.[5]

In truth, we have no precise measure of crime and delinquency in a nation. Present data on crime and delinquency give *indications*, not *measurements*.

[4]R. H. Beattie, "Problems of Criminal Statistics in the United States," *The Journal of Criminal Law, Criminology and Police Science*, 46, No. 2 (July 1955), 178.
[5]*Ibid.*

The Unreliability of Statistics

Most people probably have some general idea of what the term "crime" means, but few realize what a really broad word it is and what it encompasses. Crime, presumably, is to be defined as acts of human behavior, prohibited by law, which carry the possibility of conviction and punishment for persons engaged in such acts. Historically, almost every form of human behavior has been at some time defined as crime. Ordinarily, acts such as homicide, robbery, assault, theft, rape, burglary, arson, and kidnapping are thought of as crimes. Of those just named, most involve overt acts, easily identified, which harm either an individual or his property and are usually reported to local law enforcement authorities.

Most of the preceding acts, when committed by the youthful offender, are viewed by the juvenile court as law violations. There are many other types of human behavior, delinquent or otherwise, also defined as crimes that bear covert criminal characteristics, particularly in the fields of vice, morals, and drug and liquor use. Many such crimes, for example drug use and sale of drugs, are consensual in nature and not often reported to the police since the victim (the youthful offender included) and offender mutually benefit by concealing the joint act.

Further, within any set of acts defined as criminal, there is a problem of degree of seriousness. Certainly overt acts that are harmful and of a serious degree will be reported with high frequency; but as the degree of seriousness lessens, the probability of reporting also lessens. Obviously, the theft of an object having little value or use is *not reported* with the same degree of frequency as the theft of an item with a high value.

Crime is defined by laws of the sovereign state. The legal institutions created to control the defined problem are authorized by the same authority. Basically, law enforcement at its primary level is provided through municipal police departments and county sheriff's offices or, in some states, state police, who perform this service outside incorporated cities. The basic procedures these agencies utilize to enforce their criminal codes are:

1. to learn of crimes either through observation or reports from citizens and to investigate them as to their actuality;

The Unreliability of Statistics

2. to seek out and take into custody alleged offenders;
3. to perform general surveillance in the community that restricts, as far as possible, the incidence of criminal acts; and
4. to seek out those law violators that are generally not reported by victims and witnesses through special investigative units which combat consensual illegal activities.

It follows, therefore, that the knowledge available on the amount of crime and the offender involved is basically a matter of what the primary enforcement agencies know and record. Obviously, any measurement of crime is dependent upon the *collection, assemblage, storage, and presentation of data.* Those agencies with limited facilities and personnel for the purpose of classifying, recording, and counting criminal events generally reflect *low crime rates.* The more sophisticated record-keepers trained in crime classifications report more complete and accurate data, and they *suffer from their own exactness by comparison.*

In the United States there are over 8,000 primary law enforcement agencies. The fact that so many separate agencies are involved in these reporting procedures, coupled with the fact that crime reporting in its initial stages is never entirely complete, inevitably lead to reporting *inconsistencies.* Whether crime is even to be counted depends on the local agency's interpretation of standard instructions, as well as the particular laws governing this type of crime in the respective state.

FBI Uniform Crime Report and the U.S. Children's Bureau Statistical Series

As previously stated, there are two agencies that compile statistics on crime and delinquency in the United States. These two agencies—the Federal Bureau of Investigation and the U.S. Children's Bureau (a subsidiary of the Department of Health, Education and Welfare)—report to other agencies and the general public about crime and delinquency in the United States.

During the year 1930, by act of Congress, the Federal Bureau of Investigation was given the responsibility of carrying on the collection of data. This collection has continued without interruption to the present and is published annually in the FBI's widely known "Uniform Crime Reports." While changing little in content during the past 25 years, the Uniform Crime Reports have gradually increased in coverage so that, for the year 1969, approximately 5,000 city and county law enforcement agencies serving 125.5 million persons were submitting data to the FBI. In collecting data for these reports, the crime count is limited to seven categories. The seven major offenses are *willful homicide* (which includes murder and manslaughter, but excludes deaths arising from vehicular-type accidents), *forcible rape, robbery, aggravated assault, burglary, larceny*, and, as a special category, *auto theft*. The general larceny category has been limited in the national collection to thefts of over $50, which are counted as major offenses as opposed to lesser crimes under $50. Although the Uniform Crime Reports are fairly accurate (accurate, that is, for a statistical series), it is known that the statistical reporting in the area of juvenile delinquency is somewhat weak.

There is an agency, however, which collects rather accurate though limited statistics pertaining to juvenile crime. This agency, the U.S. Children's Bureau—Social and Rehabilitation Service, reports annually on delinquent activities in "Juvenile Court Statistics." The purpose of this service is to furnish information which will be of value to professionals in the field of law enforcement. The bureau feels that the collection and publication of such information is essential to law enforcement agencies in evaluating their programs and achieving full understanding of the crime situation and how it is handled in any given area.

According to the Children's Bureau, the *extent* of the delinquency problem in 1970 (Table 2–1) is quite significant. Nearly one million juvenile delinquency cases (excluding traffic offenses) were handled by juvenile courts in the United States in this year. The estimated number of children involved in the cases (988,500) was lower, however, since in some instances the same child was referred more than once during the year. These children represent 16% of all children aged 10 through 17 in the country.[6]

[6]Juvenile Court Statistical Series, U. S. Children's Bureau, op. cit., pp. 10–11.

Table 2–1

Number of Delinquency Cases (Excluding Traffic) Disposed
of by Juvenile Courts, United States, 1969

Type of Court	Total		Boys		Girls	
	Number	Percent	Number	Percent	Number	Percent
Total	988,500	100	760,000	100	228,500	100
Urban	646,600	66	490,000	65	156,600	68
Semi-urban	280,800	28	222,000	29	58,800	26
Rural	61,100	6	48,000	6	13,100	6

Source: U. S. Department of Health, Education and Welfare (Washington,
D. C.: U. S. Government Printing Office, 1969) p. 13.

The bureau further states that there is a definite trend
(Tables 2–2, 2–3, 2–4, and 2–5 and Figure 2–1) in 1969.
There was, again, an increase in the number of juvenile court
delinquency cases over the previous year. The increase from
1969 was 9.9 percent as compared to an increase in the child
population aged 10 through 17 of only 2.3 percent. Thus,
the upward trend in the number of delinquency cases, noted
every year since 1949, with the exception of 1961, continues.
And, again, as in most previous years in the past decade, the
increase exceeded the increase in the child population. Between 1960 and 1969, the number of juvenile court cases increased by 90 percent as compared to a 27 percent increase in
the number of children aged 10 through 17. The increase

Table 2–2

Percent Change in Delinquency Cases (Excluding Traffic)
Disposed of by Juvenile Courts, United States, 1968–1969

Type of Court	Total	Boys	Girls	Judicial	Nonjudicial
Total	+10	+7	+19	+3	+17
Urban	+10	+8	+16	+1	+18
Semi-urban	+9	+6	+24	−1	+20
Rural	+9	+4	+35	+28	−17

Source: United States Department of Health, Education and Welfare, Children's Bureau (Washington, D. C.: U. S. Government Printing Office, 1969),
p. 14.

Scope and Nature of the Problem: Measurement and Statistics

Table 2–3

Number and Rate of Delinquency Cases Disposed of by Juvenile Courts, United States, 1940–1969

Year	Delinquency Cases[a]		Rate[c]
	Including Traffic	Excluding Traffic	
1940	200,000		
1941	224,000		
1942	250,000		
1943	344,000		
1944	330,000		
1945	344,000		
1946	295,000		
1947	262,000		
1948	254,000		
1949	272,000		
1950	280,000		
1951	298,000		
1952	332,000		
1953	374,000		
1954	395,000		
1955	431,000		
1956	520,000		
1957	603,000	440,000	19.8
1958	[b] 703,000	473,000	20.1
1959	[b] 773,000	483,000	19.6
1960	813,000	510,000	20.1
1961	801,000	503,000	19.3
1962	867,000	555,000	20.5
1963	967,000	601,000	21.4
1964	1,128,000	686,000	23.5
1965	1,157,000	697,000	23.6
1966	1,268,000	745,000	24.7
1967	1,360,300	811,000	26.4
1968	1,455,000	900,000	28.7
1969	1,559,900	988,500	30.9

[a]Data for 1955–1969 estimated from the national sample of juvenile courts. Data prior to 1955 estimated by the Children's Bureau, based on reports from a comparable group of courts. Inclusion of data for Alaska and Hawaii beginning in 1960 does not materially affect the trend.
[b]Much of the increase is accounted for in one State by administrative change in the method of handling juvenile traffic cases.
[c]Based on delinquency cases (excluding traffiic) per 1,000 U. S. child population 10–17 years of age.
Source: Ibid., p. 15.

FBI Uniform Crime Report and the U.S. Children's Bureau Statistical Series

Table 2–4

Number and Percent Distribution of Delinquency Cases (Excluding Traffic) Disposed of by Juvenile Courts, by Type of Court, United States, 1958–1969

Year	Urban		Semi-urban		Rural	
	Number	Percent	Number	Percent	Number	Percent
1958	298,000	63	120,000	26	52,000	11
1959	295,000	61	127,000	26	61,000	13
1960	344,000	67	128,000	25	42,000	8
1961	350,000	69	119,000	24	34,000	7
1962	383,000	69	132,500	24	39,500	7
1963	414,000	69	146,000	24	41,000	7
1964	456,000	67	181,000	26	49,000	7
1965	470,000	68	183,500	26	43,000	6
1966	490,000	66	206,500	28	48,500	6
1967	525,000	65	235,300	29	50,700	6
1968	588,200	65	256,400	29	55,200	6
1969	646,600	66	280,800	28	61,100	6

Source: Ibid., p. 16.

Table 2–5

Number and Percent Distribution of Delinquency Cases (Excluding Traffic) Disposed of by Juvenile Courts by Manner of Handling, United States, 1958–1969

Year	Judicial		Nonjudicial	
	Number	Percent	Number	Percent
1958	237,000	50	233,000	50
1959	250,000	52	233,000	48
1960	258,000	50	256,000	50
1961	257,000	51	246,000	49
1962	285,000	51	270,000	49
1963	298,000	50	303,000	50
1964	333,000	49	353,000	51
1965	327,000	47	370,000	53
1966	357,000	48	387,000	52
1967	382,100	47	428,900	53
1968	425,400	47	474,400	53
1969	433,300	44	555,200	56

Source: Ibid., p. 17.

Scope and Nature of the Problem: Measurement and Statistics

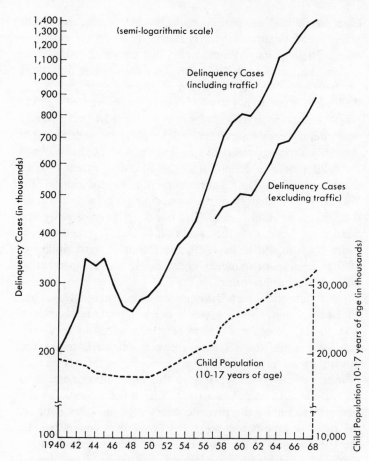

Figure 2—1. Trend in Juvenile Court Delinquency Cases and Child Population 10—17 Years of Age, 1940 to Date.

Source: U. S. Department of Health, Education and Welfare, p. 18.

in delinquency cases in 1969 was higher than the increase noted in 1968.

Nationally, according to the bureau, there was a 10.4 percent increase in boys' cases and an 11.6 percent increase in girls' cases. Among the different types of courts, however, there was no consistent pattern; in urban and rural courts girls' cases increased more than boys', but in semi-urban courts the reverse was true.

The juvenile court delinquency statistics cited here are useful mainly as an indication of how frequently the juvenile

FBI Uniform Crime Report and the U.S. Children's Bureau Statistical Series court is utilized in dealing with juvenile delinquency. Do juvenile court cases adequately reflect *trends* in the extent of juvenile delinquency? Would not police arrests of juveniles be a better indicator than court statistics, since arrest data does not have some of the limitations of juvenile court data? The Children's Bureau has found that both sources of data—police arrests of juveniles reported by the FBI and juvenile court delinquency cases reported here—show a remarkable similarity in their trends over a long period of time despite their differences in definitions, units of count, extent of coverage, and so on. Both figures surged upward during World War II, fell off sharply in the immediate post-war years, and then began to climb again. The trend has been steadily upward since 1949, with the exception of the slight decrease in court cases in 1961. In 1969, the increases were similar—10.7 percent in delinquency court cases, and 9.7 percent in police arrests of juveniles.

In juvenile court delinquency data, each offense has an equal weight. Since juvenile delinquency cases cover a wide variety of offenses—from relatively trivial to very serious—and since the offenses are not weighted, might the upward trend merely reflect an increase in the occurrence of minor offenses? In replying to this question, one needs to rely on the data on police arrests of juveniles reported by the FBI which, unlike the juvenile court data, includes data on the types of arrests and the types of offenses committed. In the 1969 edition of the Uniform Crime Reports, the FBI reported that arrests of juveniles under 18 years of age, for all types of offenses, doubled between 1960 and 1969. For a group of serious offenses selected as being most reliably reported (criminal homicide, forcible rape, burglary, robbery, aggravated assault, larceny and auto theft), the combined increase between 1960 and 1969 was 78.5 percent. When offenses against a person (homicide, forcible rape, aggravated assault, and robbery), generally accepted as being a most serious crime, are selected from the reliably reported group, the increase between 1960 and 1969 was 124.1 percent. It cannot be assumed, therefore, that the upward trend in juvenile delinquency as determined from police arrest data is due primarily to an increase in minor offenses. All groups of offenses seem to be increasing, with the most serious ones showing substantially greater increases.

Impact on Law Enforcement
Agencies

On the basis of statistical information, it is estimated that in cities with a population of over 10,000 there are 552 police departments that have specialized juvenile officers or units.[7] In 1950, there were approximately 1,348 urban places of this size (incorporated and unincorporated) in the United States. The estimated national percentage of cities of such size having specialized juvenile officers or units is 41 percent. Although it appears that there has been an increase in specialization and certainly a definite increase in manpower, studies reveal that these increases are not sufficient.[8] The tremendous rise in juvenile crime has placed a great burden on local law enforcement agencies in the area of manpower and the caliber of officers selected for juvenile specialists.

That proportionately more police departments in the smaller communities have lower educational requirements for male juvenile officers than for male recruits in the same departments might be expected. Smaller size, however, does not automatically handicap police departments in meeting suggested standards—proportionately more departments in the smaller cities required higher educational backgrounds for juvenile officer applicants than was the case in the largest city departments.[9]

Recruit training in juvenile law enforcement apparently has also felt the impact of juvenile crime. It is now generally accepted that basic training of all police officers should include some instruction in working with juveniles. This training has the effect of making every officer a juvenile officer. Indeed, one authority holds that ". . . the responsibility for disseminating knowledge about juveniles to the entire department through in-service and recruit training programs should be the duty of the juvenile unit."[10]

[7] *Juvenile Court Statistical Series*, U. S. Department of Health, Education and Welfare, *op. cit.*, pp. 17–18.

[8] *Ibid.*

[9] *Annual Reports of Federal Activities in Juvenile Delinquency, Youth Development, and Related Fields*, U. S. Department of Health, Education and Welfare (Washington, D. C.: U. S. Government Printing Office, 1971), pp. 1–7.

[10] Beattie, *op. cit.*, pp. 41–42.

The available arrest information raises more questions than it answers regarding the processing of the juvenile. We know, for example, the gross number of juveniles arrested, their sex, their age, and even their racial or ethnic breakdowns. While it would appear that the seriousness of the offense plays a key role in determining referrals to probation, we know also that the largest single group referred by police to probation are youngsters "guilty" of delinquent tendencies rather than of criminal law violations.

However, we do not know: (1) why there are gross variations in dispositions by police agencies, (2) what is meant by "handling a case within the department," (3) whether or not the referral to a probation department is by citation or delivery and detention. Further, we have no hard facts as to ethnic or socioeconomic breakdown of the various sub-population groups. Thus, there is no way of determining if or how these factors operate in determining dispositional patterns; nor will we be able to pinpoint the answers to the questions raised until we overcome the inadequacy and non-uniformity of statistical recordkeeping and data development. More uniform and adequate reporting techniques are an important prerequisite to the resolution of many other system problems as well.

As stated earlier, training for law enforcement officers has long been of major concern, especially as it relates to the juvenile court law and the general handling of juveniles. With juvenile arrests constituting a substantial portion of all arrests, simple logic would dictate that *all* police have the advantage of special training in handling children and youths; and the need for greater training capability is manifest.

Other problems and needs relate to the police practice of referring a major portion of juvenile arrestees to the probation department. In 1969, for example, California police agencies' referrals to probation were 53.1 percent of total arrests, and they accounted for 86.6 percent of all new referrals to the probation department. Of all cases on which police made referrals, approximately 93 percent were referred to probation.[11]

[11]*Crime and Delinquency in California*, Division of Criminal Law and Enforcement, Bureau of Criminal Statistics, 1969, p. 13.

Scope and Nature of the Problem: Measurement and Statistics

This wide use of probation services raises two important issues. The *first* concerns the paucity of noncorrectional community resources such as children's protective services. Most protective services bureaus are currently very small operations within the public welfare departments. The *second* issue concerns the police *policy* regarding the preponderance of these referrals to probation.

There is some reason to believe that better training in the use of other community resources, together with a policy permitting such use, could reduce the volume of probation referrals. The development and application of the police-probation citation system has generally been effective; however, the system may have helped to increase the numbers subject to formal handling. Perhaps it should be expanded to allow police to cite juveniles and their parents to other departments and agencies, both public and private.

There is a pressing need for law enforcement to engage in more positive interchange with the community at large and children and youth specifically. Through positive action programs by police, communication with the community could be established, the public image of the police could be enhanced, and increased acceptance and respect for law could be achieved.

Summary

Chapter 2 discusses the limitations relating to the measurement of delinquent activity in the United States. One major limitation in regard to the increase in juvenile crime is imposed by the fact that statistical evaluation of juvenile delinquency is relatively new—approximately 15 to 20 years old. Therefore, since earlier statistics are not available, it is impossible to make a definitive statement regarding the significance of the increase in this problem. Another factor relating to the increase in delinquent activity—and all statistical information points to a definite increase when compared to the growth of the youth population—is the fact that police are apprehending and taking into custody more juveniles. The third factor is that police are arresting juveniles today for activities that were not considered serious in previous years.

Most of the criminal statistics in the United States are

compiled by the Federal Bureau of Investigation. This data is published periodically in the FBI's Uniform Crime Reports. Although the Uniform Crime Reports are fairly accurate in reporting the number of crimes committed and other pertinent data pertaining to juvenile crime, they do not report on court dispositions. Actual court appearances and dispositions are reported by the Department of Health, Education and Welfare in the form of an annual report submitted by the Children's Bureau—Social and Rehabilitation Service.

The final area covered in this chapter concerns the impact of juvenile crime on law enforcement agencies throughout the United States. It is generally accepted that most law enforcement agencies have found it necessary to increase their staff and provide specialized services to handle the increase in youthful crime.

Selected References

BEATTIE, R. H., "Problems of Criminal Statistics in the United States," *The Journal of Law, Criminology and Police Science*, 46, No. 2 (July 1955), 177–79.

CRESSY, D. R., "The State of Criminal Statistics," *NPPA Journal*, 3, No. 3 (July 1967), 230–41.

GIBBONS, D. C., *Delinquent Behavior*, Chap. 1. Englewood Cliffs, N. J.: Prentice-Hall, Inc., 1970.

GRIFFIN, J. I., *Statistics Essential for Police Efficiency*, Chaps. 1 and 2. Springfield, Ill.: Charles C Thomas, Publisher, 1958.

LEJINS, P. J., "American Data on Juvenile Delinquency in an International Forum," *Federal Probation*, 25, No. 18 (June 1961), 19.

TAFT, D., *Criminology* (3rd ed.), Chap. 4. New York: The Macmillan Company, 1956.

Understanding Delinquent Behavior

Delinquents do not just happen. They are the products of circumstance and chance, culture and environment, and—most important—sociological and psychological conditioning. It is out of one or a combination of these factors that delinquency usually grows. Let us examine the role of each of them briefly.

Circumstance and Chance: A small number of youths acquire the label delinquent by circumstance. These young people require neither the skilled help nor the extensive treatment that delinquents influenced by other factors may need. Given temporary assistance and guidance, they will return to patterns of normal and acceptable behavior. Frequently, the young person who commits a delinquent act by chance is a member of a group that engages in unlawful behavior temporarily. It is the presence and pressure of his friends and associates that helps "Johnny" commit an act which he knows is wrong. This type of offender is similar to the "statistical delinquent" previously discussed in connection with the police concept of delinquency.

Culture and Environment: Youths who reside in areas of crime and vice often learn to esteem lawlessness and engage in crime and delinquency because it is the acceptable thing to do. In such areas, the cultural delinquent is trained to value many things that the greater society rejects. He is not maladjusted in the usual sense. He sees nothing wrong with the values he holds, hence is unable to grasp the significance of his illegal behavior. All of his values may not be at odds with the greater society; it may well be that only a few important ones are inconsistent and unacceptable.

chapter
3

The cultural delinquent has a greater opportunity than other youths to get into trouble. He not only lives with crime and vice, but also faces a greater chance for apprehension by the large concentration of law enforcement officers in his community. Even if this youth holds to the values that the greater society accepts, his potential for delinquency is enhanced by the area in which he resides.

Psychological Conditioning: Many children have been psychologically conditioned to have high delinquency potentials. These children often become delinquents long before they receive official recognition by the police and courts. In this group, we find children who have had everything they have done or said disapproved. Every effort has been made to make them feel inferior. Their parents have denied them admiration, appreciation, and affection. Often they have been permitted to express their desires and have even had these desires stimulated by responsible adults who later "squelched" them. In addition to having had little of what they needed, children in this group have frequently been punished, or at least accused of, things they did not do. Their parents and other adults have shown constant suspicion and disbelief of their actions and intentions. Further, the parents have usually demanded absolute obedience without explanation and have refused to permit self-expression.

Psychogenic delinquency has its roots in these unhealthy relationships between children and the adult figures in their lives. The child who becomes antisocial because of such relationships tend to display marked characteristics as a potential delinquent. He is socially aggressive and shows extremes in defiance, suspicion, and destructiveness. His emotional ups and downs fluctuate without apparent cause. Most children are adventurous. The delinquent, however, is overly adventurous and extremely outgoing, demanding, and aggressive in his social relationships. He is also susceptible and is easily lead by children in his own group when he accepts them as his authority. When with adults and others in authority, however, he is frequently stubborn.

All children exhibit such symptoms at some time or another. Growing up is an uneven process with many ups and downs. In the case of the delinquent child, the symptoms are exaggerated and become established patterns for doing business with adults. It is the extent and duration of the deviations that establish delinquency, not just a single unusual or illegal action by a child. Because of his psychological conditioning, a child may possess a high delinquency potential. The delinquency, however, may never be expressed unless certain necessary conditions exist, for example, opportunity and ability to engage in unacceptable behavior.

Children who exhibit the initial characteristics of delinquency are the product of situations, environments, and/or families whose carelessness and lack of concern provide the fertile soil in which delinquency thrives. Delinquents don't just happen, they are unfortunately molded into a definite form of deviant behavior.

Explanations of
Delinquent Behavior

Of all the social ailments which plague American society, none has aroused more deeply felt concern—and more anguished but misled editorial and official comment—than the phenomenon of juvenile delinquency. And no other concern of the social sciences, including problems such as divorce, labor-management conflict, ethnic and racial prejudice, poverty, and drug addiction, has given rise to more contradictory viewpoints so vigorously expressed. In an attempt to cut through the emotion surrounding the problem, and to better understand its sources, this chapter examines some theories of deviant behavior as they relate to the delinquent.

Deviant behavior has been seen in many different ways throughout history. Generally, the various theories of deviant behavior fall into three categories: (1) deterministic deviance, (2) self-determined deviance, and (3) a combination of self-determined and deterministic deviance. *Deterministic theories* view the deviate as a person who either has no control over his own behavior, or is grossly influenced by external or internal factors. Theories of *self-determined deviance*, on the other hand, see the deviate as a person who has complete control over his own behavior. The third group of theories sees the delinquent as a person who is to *some extent controlled by external or internal influences, but who also exercises a degree of self-control.*

From these three basic positions, numerous "explanations" of deviant behavior have evolved. Insofar as they relate

Understanding Delinquent Behavior

35

to "self-deterministic" deviance, such explanations generally narrow down to a belief that insufficient punishment is the "cause" of deviance. But those that relate to "deterministic" deviance offer a wide variety of "explanations" for deviant behavior. For purposes here, these explanations will be classified as *sociological, personality disorder*, and *physiological* explantions. Of course there is considerable overlap between the three categories, although they will be discussed separately in this chapter.

Sociological Explanations

Many of the deterministic explanations of deviance draw on theories that are called: the *cultural approach* (i.e., influences of various social values, statuses, roles, social structures, etc.); or the *social approach* (i.e., factors dealing with family and marital status, education, recreation, religion, occupation, etc.). For the sake of simplicity, both of these approaches will be discussed under the broader classification of "Sociological Explanations."

Cultural Approach

Perceptive observers contend that the United States is in many respects the oldest country on earth because it has more experience with the complexities of modern industrial society than any other nation. This experience has included the development of a youth subculture that remains, for the time being at least, more or less peculiar to the United States.

The idea of referring to a given age group as a subculture suggests classification of the term culture itself. Some 160 social science definitions of the term culture have been reduced by the author to the following:

> Culture consists of patterns, explicit and implicit, by symbols, constituting the distinctive achievement of human groups, including their embodiment and artifacts; the essential core of culture consists of traditional ideas and their attached values; culture systems may on the one hand be considered as products of action, on the other hand as conditioning elements of further action.

Understanding Delinquent Behavior

A subculture, therefore, could simply be a group at variance (or deviance) with the broad culture's "patterns . . . artifacts . . . traditional ideas . . . ," and so on. Of course, there could be subcultures that were not necessarily "at variance" (or at deviance). However, a subculture at considerable variance with the larger culture was what criminologist Albert Cohen had in mind when he wrote his book, *Delinquent Boys*.[1] The variance (or deviance) of the gang subculture is in part attributed by Cohen to the "significantly different social worlds" between middle-class children and working-class children as they grow up. As the working-class child experiences frustration in achievement of culturally desirable goals, the readily available alternatives emerge.

The frustration of working-class children is identified by many cultural theorists as a struggle between "means and ends." Put another way, highly competitive struggling for material wealth eventually narrows the number of possible "victors" when "victory" is only attainable through *legitimate means*. It follows then that youths who lack the cultural advantage of legitimate means (that are often acquired through neighborhood and family status) are likely to experience frustration in competition with youths who are fortunate enough to have access to legitimate means. The reaction of those who are culturally denied in this manner (often referred to as "have-nots") is to develop *illegitimate means* which, in turn, becomes defined by the broad culture as deviance.

An interesting extension of this theoretical explanation of deviance was posed by criminologist Edwin H. Sutherland.[2] Calling his theory *differential association*, Sutherland concluded that deviance flows from excessive exposure to social codes that prove conducive to misconduct. A person constantly exposed to deviance and rarely exposed to cultural conformity may well come to conceive of deviance as "normal." Another criminologist, Walter Reckless, elaborates certain implications of differential association by noting that a child growing up in a setting where he learns the technique and "justifications" for deviant behavior will respond to this influence in the same manner as a middle-class child respond-

---

[1] A. H. Cohen, *Delinquent Boys* (New York: The Free Press, 1955).

[2] E. H. Sutherland and D. R. Cressey, *Principles of Criminology*, 5th. ed. (Philadelphia, Pa.: J. B. Lippincott Co., 1955).

Sociological Explanations

ing to the influences of culturally accepted patterns of behavior.[3] To Reckless, the process of a child acquiring either
the culture or the subculture is identical—only the *content*
differs.

Criminologists have also related the theory of differential
association to middle-class deviance, but the actual process
remains essentially the same. Stress is laid on the frequency
and the intimacy of social influences.

Social Approach

The family, particularly the parent, is a crucial aspect
of the juvenile probation department's corrective treatment.
This acknowledgement of the importance of the family unit
implies that an intact marriage supports juvenile corrective
goals.

The earliest juvenile courts noted that nearly 50 percent
of delinquents came from broken homes, and they did not
take long to blame divorce and desertion for the problem of
juvenile delinquency.[4] Subsequently, studies were made in
an effort to estimate the proportion of broken homes in the
general population as compared to families of delinquents.
Criminologists Shaw and McKay found that only 42.5 percent of delinquent children came from broken homes, and
they interpreted their findings as evidence that broken homes,
although significant, were not a main "cause" of juvenile
deviance.[5]

However, later studies of the relationship between
broken homes and juvenile deviance tended to support the
contention that broken homes and delinquency are related.
Indeed, a study of some 44,448 Philadelphian delinquents
found a definite and continuous decline in the percentage of
delinquents who live with both parents.[6]

[3]W. C. Reckless, *The Crime Problem*, 2nd. ed. (New York: Appleton-
Century-Crofts, 1955).

[4]H. M. Shulman, *Juvenile Deliquency in American Society* (New York:
Harper & Row, Publishers; 1961), pp. 391–92.

[5]C. R. Shaw and H. D. McKay, *Juvenile Delinquency in Urban Areas*
(Chicago: University of Chicago Press, 1942).

[6]T. P. Monahan, "Family Status and the Delinquent Child," *Social
Forces*, Vol. 35 (March 1959), pp. 250–58.

The nature of the parental separation has also been studied. It was found that desertion, divorce, and separation while one parent is in prison tends to be associated with juvenile delinquency. Where separation is due to a death or serious illness of one parent, there is statistically less incidence of juvenile deviance.

Another "social variable" thought to be related to juvenile deviance is recreation, or perhaps the lack of recreation. Studies have indicated that delinquents seek exciting diversions which often occur on dark streets, vacant lots, and railroad yards. Delinquent acts themselves become recreation for the youths involved, although some criminologists believe that delinquent activities serving as recreation are merely a "transition" to delinquency for profit. But whether or not such recreation is a "transition," Sheldon and Eleanor Glueck in their book, *Unraveling Juvenile Delinquency*,[7] reported that delinquents are more outgoing and active than non-delinquents—findings that suggest that recreational-type diversion is at least one variable of juvenile deviance.

The national economy itself is another variable thought by many criminologists to at least partially explain deviance. However, the late Paul Tappan questioned the relationship between deviant behavior and the national economy by noting the vast majority of economically impoverished families who did not become involved in deviant behavior.[8] The social forces which stress economic solutions to deviance nevertheless continue to gain prominence in efforts to reduce deviant behavior.

Personality Maladjustment Approach

Many psychiatrically-oriented criminologists consider delinquency a product of *personality maladjustment*. They see the socialization process as producing rather healthy or un-

[7] S. Glueck and E. Glueck, *Unraveling Juvenile Delinquency* (New York: Commonwealth Fund, 1950).

[8] P. W. Tappan, *Juvenile Delinquency* (New York: McGraw-Hill Book Company, 1962).

healthy personalities and consider delinquency as a correlate of the latter.

Dr. Franz Alexander, a celebrated psychoanalyst, contends that the human being enters the world as a criminal—in other words, socially not well adjusted. "The criminal," Alexander states, "carries out in his actions in *natural*, unbridled, but instinctual drives; he acts as the child would act if it only could." He concludes that the only difference between the criminal and the normal individual is that the normal man partially controls his criminal drives and finds outlets for them in socially harmless activities.[9]

If we start with such a conception of human nature, then our problem is not to explain crime but rather its *absence*. We must now ask what, if any, are the reasons why some individuals have enough inhibitory mechanisms to refrain from transgressions while others lack these prohibitory functions? Most of the psychoanalytical writers acknowledge the relevance of the "social fact," but they tend to see it as a circumstance that triggers or precipitates a delinquent impulse that is already fully formed, but latent (lying hidden and undeveloped beneath the surface). As previously stated, such inborn or instinctual antisocial impulses are commonly referred to as the *id*; most people, in growing up, acquire a capacity for controlling these id-forces known as the *ego*. The *superego* constitutes something akin to the conscience—an inhibitor of the id drives.

A number of personality disorders which some people think have very little bearing on delinquency are considered by others to be somewhat "causal" in nature. Mental deficiency is probably one such disorder. The mentally deficient person is subnormal in that his mind has failed to develop normally, while other disorders such as psychotic conditions are abnormal in that disease or other malfunctions affect the working of the mind. Various forms of pathology and deterioration associated with psychosis may produce mental deficiency. Mental deficiency itself probably explains very little deviance except that it places the feebleminded person in an unfavorable position in a competitive society.

[9]H. E. Barnes and N. K. Teeters, *New Horizons in Criminology*, 3rd. ed. (Englewood Cliffs, N. J.: Prentice-Hall, Inc., 1959).

Understanding Delinquent Behavior

Most psychoses, and psychoneuroses for that matter, are rarely considered explanations of delinquency. However, the personality disorder known as *psychopathy* (or sociopathy) is thought by many criminologists to "cause" a great deal of deviant behavior.

A psychopathic personality can be identified in terms of four criteria: (1) a lack of conscience (or Freudian super-ego) which in turn reduces or eliminates guilt feelings regarding misconduct; (2) most or all aggressive feelings directed outward towards the world rather than inward towards one's self; (3) an infantile demand for immediate rather than postponed satisfaction of basic drives; and (4) an inability or unwillingness to form affectional bonds with others.

The actual development of psychopathy is complex but may be explained in part in terms of child discipline technique. Discipline, more often than not, seeks to inhibit the id drives in order to produce a "civilized socialization." But to inhibit basic drives requires first a consistency in discipline, and then a consistency in affection. Consistency in affection is needed to insure that "guilt feelings" occur when id impulses go unchecked. A kind of "bribery" is involved in which the parent (often the mother) threatens withdrawal of love if the child fails to relinquish his id drives. However, the child *without* feelings of maternal love is unlikely to feel threatened by the withdrawal of what he does not feel exists in the first place. The guilt feelings needed to control behavior are, therefore, not forthcoming, and the psychopathic personality begins to emerge.

The problem of *alcoholism* and, perhaps, *drug dependence* (as avenues of escape from painful "reality") are thought by some to demonstrate personality disorders uniquely vulnerable to deviance. There is little agreement on how alcoholic problems develop, but a common explanation has evolved: The alcoholic tends to be "self-pampering" and he resists unpleasant states of mind while insisting on self-expression. He is unwilling to work toward attaining self-expression but tends to assume a *right* to self-expression. The alcoholic because of an imitative characteristic, developed during childhood, tends to strive for excitement which gives him a great deal of euphoria and encourages endangerment at the same time reducing his ability to use good judgment.

Physiological Explanations

Two other deterministic explanations of deviance might be called the *anthropological approach* and the *hereditary approach*. Each of these will be considered as a segment of the broader classification, "Physiological Explanations."

Anthropological Approach

The great philosopher Aristotle commented on the relationship between behavior and body type: "There was never an animal with the form of one kind and the mental characteristic of another." Even before Aristotle, medicine's ancestor, Hippocrates, described two body types relating to specific diseases. However, the first attempt to relate the body to deviance did not occur until the nineteenth century when the Italian physician and criminologist, Cesare Lombroso, sought to correlate physical features and misconduct.

Drawing heavily on phrenology (a belief that the shape and protuberances of the skull determined personality) and Darwin's theory of evolution, Lombroso sought to demonstrate what he called a "stigmata of degeneration" in which observable asymmetric physical characteristics indicated the probability of deviance.[10] The Lombrosian belief that "lantern jaws and pointed ears" might relate to deviance continued for some time to command the interests of criminologists.

In 1925, a book by Ernest Kretchmer proved to be the foundation of criminologist William H. Sheldon's systematic efforts to relate deviance to the shape of bodies.[11] Delinquents were classified by Sheldon as either *endomorph* (i.e., rotund with excessive fatty tissue); *mesomorph* (i.e., muscular); and *ectomorph* (i.e., lean and angular). Sheldon theorized that the fatter endomorphs were gregarious and affectionate and had less of a problem with deviant behavior than persons of medium build. The muscular mesomorphs were seen as delinquency-prone because of their drive for an excessive amount of physical activity. Later research by the Gluecks tended to corroborate Sheldon's reasoning and, to this day, a mesomorphic body type is considered by many to count at

[10]D. R. Taft, *Criminology*, 3rd. ed. (New York: The Macmillan Company, 1956), pp. 62–63.
[11]*Ibid.*

least in part for deviance.[12] Finally, the tall, lean, often nervous ectomorphs were seen as shy and aloof and, therefore, not prone to deviance.

Hereditary Approach

Students of criminology are invariably confronted with studies made of three seemingly criminal families: the *Jukes*, the *Kallikaks*, and the *Nams*. The legendary criminality of the Jukes and the Kallikaks is customarily cited as evidence of deviance being "inherited" like other family characteristics. The sociological "environmentalists," of course, pose the traditional counter-argument that the very process of being reared in a criminal atmosphere leads to deviance.

Biologist M. F. Ashley Montague seems to combine environmental and hereditary influences by acknowledging both "cultural factors" along with "the genetically determined, nervous, methological individual."[13] Somewhat surprisingly for a biologist, Montague sees *culture* as being possibly more significant than heredity in determining behavioral patterns. The field of criminology in general continues to reserve judgment on hereditary considerations in deviate behavior until research clarifies questions such as: What is the significance of the high percentage of abnormal electroencephelographs among delinquents? How much do we really know of the birth of the delinquent and that all important first 15 minutes of life? The picture will remain confused until we can answer these questions and many others.

Summary

This chapter attempts to develop understanding of some of the basic causes of delinquency. The chapter presents a number of theories which seek to explain the problem in three general categories: *sociological explanations, personality maladjustment explanations*, and *physiological explanations*.

Some of the theories included in the discussion are:

[12]*Ibid.*
[13]Barnes and Teeters, op. cit.

Albert Cohen's *gang subculture*; Edwin Sutherland's *differential association*, and its expansion by Walter Reckless; Sheldon and Eleanor Glueck's theory relating to recreational diversion; Paul Tappan's theory regarding the relationship between deviant behavior and the national economy; and the theory of Franz Alexander, the celebrated psychoanalyst, and David Abrahamsen, a noted psychiatrist.

The chapter's energies are directed toward integrating the many contributions of different social science disciplines —most notably sociology, cultural anthropology, social psychology, clinical psychology, criminology, and social psychiatry—into a meaningful overall explanation of the causes of delinquency.

Selected References

BARNES, H. E., and N. K. TEETERS, *New Horizons in Criminology* (3rd ed.), Chaps. 1–5. Englewood Cliffs, N. J.: Prentice-Hall, Inc., 1959.

BARRON, M., *The Juvenile in Delinquent Society*, Chap. 4. New York: Alfred A. Knopf, Inc., 1954.

BLOCH, H. A., and F. FLYNN, *Delinquency: The Juvenile Offender in America Today*, pp. 205–19. New York: Random House, Inc., 1956.

BORDUA, D., "Delinquent Subcultures: Sociological Interpretations of Gang Delinquency," *The Annals of the American Academy of Political and Social Science*, Vol. 338, Nov. 1961, pp. 119–36.

ELDEFONSO, E., A. COFFEY, and R. C. GRACE, *Principles of Law Enforcement*, Chap. 3. New York: John Wiley & Sons, Inc., 1968.

GLUECK, S., and E. GLUECK, *Unraveling Juvenile Delinquency*, pp. 166–67. New York: Commonwealth Fund, 1950.

Juvenile Court: Its Purposes, Functions, and Operation

Like all other institutions in our rapidly evolving democratic society, the juvenile court is undergoing change. It is changing as a system, as an agency of government, and as a social service to meet the diverse needs of the many different courts, communities, and individuals which it exists to serve.

The juvenile court has become the primary judicial agency for dealing with juvenile criminality, the single most pressing and threatening aspect of the crime problem in the United States. In order to realize the impact of youthful crime on the juvenile court system of today, one need only refer to the statistics presented in Chapter 2. These statistics indicate that responsibility for meeting the problems of crime rests more heavily on the juvenile court than on any other judicial institution in our society.

To fulfill this responsibility, the juvenile court cannot be isolated from the rest of the community's treatment facilities. It is an integral part, perhaps the most important part, of the formal treatment picture. Its function is to diagnose the problem, to prescribe treatment both within and without the court, and then to see to it that the treatment is carried out. The fundamental idea of the juvenile court law

chapter

4

is that the state must step in and exercise guardianship over a child who is a victim of adverse social or individual conditions which develop crime. The law proposes a plan whereby he may be treated, not as a criminal legally charged with a crime, but as a ward of the state, to receive virtually the same care, custody, and discipline that are accorded the neglected and dependent child and which, as the Juvenile court Act of that respective state dictates, "shall approximate as nearly as may be that which should be given by his parents."[1]

Development of the Juvenile Court

The juvenile court emerged from the conflux of many different practices and thoughts, some of which were centuries old, others relatively recent responses to our rapidly changing society and social conditions.

Originally, the concept of the juvenile court was derived from the English courts which had differential treatment for children. The best known source of the idea of the juvenile court is summed up in the Latin phrase, *parens patriae*. The English concept of the king in the role of parent was the basis of the *parens patriae* theory accepted in the United States as the foundation of the juvenile court.

As *parens patriae*, the state, substituting for the king, invested the juvenile court with the power to act as parent of the child. The judge was to assume a fatherly role, protecting the juvenile in order to cure and save him. The juvenile court withheld from the child the procedural safeguards granted to adults because it viewed him as having the right to custody rather than the right to liberty, and juvenile proceedings were civil, not criminal.[2]

When the English legal system was transplanted to the United States, the activities of the Court of Chancery were

[1]*Welfare and Institution's Code*, State of California, Sacramento, California, 1971.

[2]C. E. Reasons, "Gault: Procedural Change and Substantive Effect," *Crime and Delinquency*, 16, No. 2 (Apr. 1970), 164.

Juvenile Court: Its Purpose, Functions, and Operation

extended to include protection of minors in danger of personal as well as property injury, and it is as inheritor of this court's protective powers that the juvenile court in the United States has most commonly been justified against Constitutional attack.

The Court of Chancery, however, dealt only with neglected and dependent children, not with children accused of criminal law violations, and the historical basis of the present-day juvenile court's delinquency jurisdiction has been a matter of some dispute. But such jurisdiction seems to have had its logical justification in the failure of the older criminal courts to prevent crime and their inability to experiment with more effective judicial methods and procedures. Another rationale for the assumption of the present-day juvenile court's delinquency jurisdiction lies in the social sciences. The social sciences were regarded as capable of identifying methods of appropriate treatment for youthful offenders, and an emphasis upon social and behavioral sciences became a major force in the juvenile court. Social resource was seen as an integral part of the judicial process.[3]

The social conditions then prevailing in the nineteenth century played an important role in intensifying the movement for reform in the treatment of children. During the nineteenth century, industrialization and immigration were driving millions of people into the cities, resulting in over-crowding, disruption of family life, increasing vice and crime, and all the other destructive factors characteristic of rapid urbanization. Because of these factors, delinquency—and those activities associated with delinquency, such as youthful incorrigible behavior, truancy, gang delinquency, curfew violations, and malicious mischief—rose rapidly and society became duly concerned about its youth. Along with the detrimental factors in urbanization, there was a rising concern throughout the nineteenth century about the official treatment of children—the growth of what has been called the spirit of social justice. The ascending social sciences, with their optimistic claims to diagnose and treat the problems underlying deviance, seemed to provide the ideal tool for implementing the dual goals of treating wayward children humanely and offsetting their deleterious surroundings.

[3]Ibid., p. 164.

From the very beginning, the juvenile court movement was given impetus when philanthropic men and women such as the members of the Chicago Women's Club, emancipated intellectual feminists like the Hull House Group, and professional penologists and reformers joined forces to achieve recognition of the greater vulnerability and salvageability of children. Initially, they sought the creation of separate institutions for youth and the substitution of non-institutional supervision whenever feasible. They then fought for physically separate court proceedings and change in the very philosophy underlying judicial handling of children.[4]

The Juvenile Court, then, was born in an aura of reform, and it spread with amazing speed. The conception of the delinquent as a "wayward child" first specifically came to life in April, 1899, when the Illinois legislature passed the Juvenile Court Act, creating the first statewide court specially for children. It did not create a new court; it did include most of the features that have since come to distinguish the juvenile court. The original act and the amendments to it that shortly followed brought together under one jurisdiction cases of dependency, neglect, and delinquency —the less comprehending incorrigibles and children threatened by immoral associations as well as criminal law breakers. Hearings were to be informal and non-public, records confidential, children detained apart from adults, a probation staff appointed. In short, children were not to be treated as criminals nor dealt with by the process used for criminals.

A new vocabulary symbolized the aura: Petition instead of complaint, summons instead of warrant, initial hearing instead of arraignment, findment of involvement instead of conviction, disposition instead of sentence. The physical surroundings were important too: They should seem less imposing than a courtroom, with the judge at a desk or table instead of behind a bench, fatherly and sympathetic while still authoritative and sovereign. The goals were to investigate, diagnose and prescribe treatment, not to adjudicate guilt or fix blame. The individual's background was more important than the facts of a given incident, specific conduct relevant more as symptomatic of a need for the

[4]Task Force Report: Juvenile Delinquency and Youth Crime, The President's Commission on Law Enforcement and Administration of Justice (Washington, D. C.: Government Printing Office, 1967), p. 2.

court to bring its helping powers to bear than as a prerequisite to emphasize jurisdiction. Lawyers were unnecessary—adversary tactics were out of place, for the mutual aim of all was not to contest or object but to determine the treatment plan best for the child. The plan was to be devised by the increasingly popular psychologists and psychiatrists; delinquency was thought of almost as a disease, to be diagnosed by specialists and the patient kindly but firmly diagnosed.[5]

Juvenile courts, at that time during the nineteenth century, were in somewhat the same position as federal courts, relatively free from criticism. Criticism was not likely to erupt unless certain practices defeated their own purposes. The courts were able to exercise a range of discretion not available or allowed in adult criminal courts. This freedom of operation continued until recent years. The subsequent change to procedural safeguards, which will be described later in this chapter, was largely due to the efforts of the school of legal realism, which views the judicial process as one in which the judge makes the law.

Juvenile Court Jurisdiction

The jurisdiction of the juvenile court is *equity jurisdiction*, the jurisdiction of the English Court of Chancery, which represents the King as *parens patriae* with respect to children. The juvenile court thus has five characteristics of equity jurisdiction:

1. *It is relatively informal in its procedure*—a characteristic going back to the origin of English equity, when one who sought relief in equity presented to the Chancellor an English bill, that is an informal petition in English, whereas one who sought relief in a court of law had to buy a Latin writ and follow it up with a formal statement of his case (called a declaration), likewise in Latin.
2. *As with all equity jurisdiction, it is remedial not punitive.*
3. *It acts preventively in advance of any specific wrongdoing.*

[5]*Ibid.*, p. 3.

4. *It employs administrative rather than adversary methods.*
5. *It can adapt its action to the circumstances of individual cases and so achieve a high degree of individualization, which is demanded by justice, if not always by security.*[6]

Juvenile courts are tribunals that deal in special ways with young people's cases. They exist in all jurisdictions. The cases they deal with include delinquency (conduct in violation of the criminal code and also truancy, ungovernability, and certain conduct illegal only for children), neglected, and abused children. The young people they deal with are those below a designated age, usually set between 16 and 21; their authority extends until the youth reaches his majority. They differ from adult and criminal courts in a number of basic respects, reflecting the philosophy that erring children should be protected and rehabilitated rather than subjected to the harshness of the criminal system.

Characteristics of the Juvenile Courts

As might be expected, juvenile courts vary in philosophy, procedure, and facilities from state to state. In fact, one may find variations among the courts from county to county within the same state.

In a strict sense, it is incorrect to speak of a juvenile court or a juvenile court system as if juvenile courts throughout the country were uniform in their structure, philosophy, and activities. To assume such uniformity would be wrong, for it is not found throughout the country or even within a single state. For example, in the first interim report of the Special Study Commission on Juvenile Justice in the State of California, published February 2, 1959, the following observations are made:

There is considerable diversity in practice among the 58 counties of this state in terms of law enforcement procedures, probation functions, and juvenile court processes and decisions. As a result, whether or not a juvenile is arrested, placed in detention, or referred to the probation

[6]R. Pound, "The Juvenile Court and the Law," *Crime and Delinquency*, 10, No. 4 (Oct. 1964), 448–49.

department, and whether or not the petition is dismissed, probation is granted, or a Youth Authority commitment is ordered by the Juvenile Court, seems to depend more upon the community in which the offense is committed than upon intrinsic merits of the individual case. . . . There is not only variation in practices among the 58 counties, but equally varied is the nature and extent of services provided juveniles by probation, law enforcement and juvenile court judges.[7]

However, although wide variations in regard to philosophy, procedure, and functions exist among juvenile courts, there are certain important traits that all have in common. The proceedings are divided into three stages. The *prejudicial stage*, commonly referred to as the "detention hearing," is the first stage. The *jurisdictional hearing* is the second stage, during which the facts are established by presentation of evidence and testimony. The last stage is the *dispositional hearing*. After jurisdiction is established, the court must decide what action would be most likely to help the juvenile avoid further difficulties. From the time he is placed in custody, the stages must comply with a definite time schedule.

From the "doctrine of *parens patriae*," the term ward or wardship has been adopted to describe youngsters who are found to come within the courts' jurisdiction. Black defines a ward as "a person, especially an infant, placed by authority of law under care of a guardian."[8]

The terms are utilized to encompass a wide range of cases referred to juvenile courts. The law violator who steals a candy bar is to be theoretically given as much consideration as one who burglarizes a house. The courts' major concern is to be focused on the reasons for the juvenile's action and how to prevent recurrence.

The structure of the juvenile court and its position or status in the state's organizational pattern vary among and even within states. Relatively few juvenile courts are separate, independent courts. Most are part of a circuit, district, superior, county, common pleas, probate, or municipal court. In a few jurisdictions, family courts have been established to

[7]*Special Commission on Juvenile Justice in the State of California,* State Printing Office, Sacramento, California Feb. 2, 1959, pp. 1–2.

[8]H. Black, *Black's Law Dictionary* (New York: West Publishing Co., 1968), p. 1754.

deal with both children's cases and domestic relation cases. Even where the jurisdiction of juvenile cases is in a court that is organizationally part of a larger system, however, the judge assigned to hear children's cases often operates his court quite independently.

It is worth reiterating that although there is variation among and in some instances within states in the jurisdiction of the juvenile courts, jurisdiction generally includes *delinquency, neglect,* and *child abuse* cases. Delinquency involves cases of children alleged to have committed an offense that if committed by an adult would be a crime. It also covers cases of children alleged to have violated specific ordinances or regulatory laws that apply only to children, such as curfew regulations, school attendance laws, restrictions on use of alcohol and tobacco, and children variously designated as beyond control, ungovernable, incorrigible, runaway, or in need of supervision. According to national juvenile court statistics, the latter two groups account for over 25 percent of the total number of delinquent children appearing before juvenile courts and between 25 and 30 percent of the population of state institutions for delinquent children. In addition to the cases of delinquent, neglected, and dependent children, juvenile courts may deal with other types of actions involving children: adoption, termination of parental rights, appointment of a guardian of the person of a minor, custody, contributing to delinquency or neglect, and non-support.[9]

In some states, major offenses such as capital crimes are excluded from a juvenile court's jurisdiction. In other states, the jurisdiction of the juvenile court is concurrent with that of the criminal court in more serious offenses.

Referrals and Procedural Requirements

In most states statutes determine procedural requirements by the police and the juvenile court. For example, statutes in the State of California set forth the manner in which a minor is handled by the police and probation officer. Section 626 of the California Welfare and Institutions Code, as an illustration, describes the procedure to be used by the police officer after arrest.

[9]*Task Force Report: Juvenile Delinquency and Crime,* p. 4.

If a minor under 18 is arrested, the procedure for disposition is as follows:

1. He may release the minor.
2. He may cite the minor to appear before the Probation Officer. The procedure for citing is as follows:
   a. Prepare in duplicate a written notice to appear before the Probation Officer.
   b. The notice should contain a concise statement on the violation and the reason why the minor was taken into custody (facts making up a violation of law).
   c. A copy of this notice is to be given to the minor or parents, and each may be required to sign a promise to appear, and the minor must then be immediately released.
   d. As soon as practicable, one copy of the notice to appear, including the facts of the offense, shall be filed with the Probation Officer.
3. The arresting officer must take the minor without unnecessary delay before the Probation Officer of the county and deliver custody of such minor to the Probation Officer.

In determining which of the three dispositions he will make, the arresting officer shall select the one which *least restricts* the minor's freedom of movement, providing such is compatible with the best interests of the minor and the community.

Most juveniles who appear in juvenile court are sent there by the police. Extensive screening and informal adjustment by the police on the street and in the police stations significantly reduce the number of apprehended juveniles referred to the court. Parents, social agencies, and others may also have recourse to the court.

Juvenile court statutes frequently provided that, when a complaint is received, the court shall make a preliminary inquiry to determine whether the interests of the child or the public require court action. The inquiry may vary from cursory investigation to full-fledged social study involving contact with numerous persons and agencies in the community. It may include a hearing at which the child, his parents, and their attorney representing the child are present. In many juvenile courts, especially the larger metropolitan ones, the preliminary screening function, known as *intake*,

Juvenile Court Jurisdiction

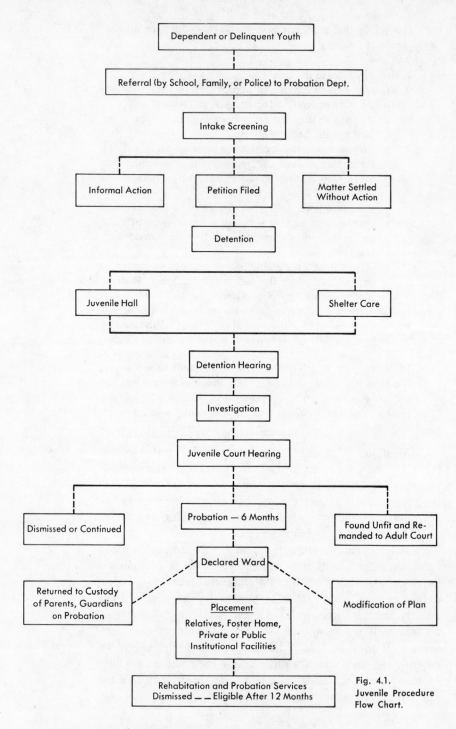

Fig. 4.1.
Juvenile Procedure
Flow Chart.

Juvenile Court: Its Purpose, Functions, and Operation

54

is performed by a special division of the probation department. Depending upon his judgment as to basis for the court's jurisdiction, sufficiency of evidence, and desirability of court action, the intake officer may dismiss the case, authorize the filing of a petition, or, in many courts, dispose of the case by "informal adjustment."

During the past five years, there have been many significant changes in juvenile court law and procedures. Most of the changes and, in some cases, important clarifications have been brought about by judicial decisions. Because of the direct relationship these court decisions have upon the police officer, a capsule summary of the pertinent changes or clarifications of the juvenile court law is appropriate at this juncture.[10]

Recent Changes in Juvenile Court Law

Civil or Criminal Hearings

One of the confusing and unanswered questions in juvenile court law is whether proceedings are to be continued as a civil hearing or to operate as a criminal hearing. Much discretion is allowed through the statute; and, as the following illustrates, the courts have generally upheld the statute in the past.

> The proceeding is civil in nature and not a conviction, nor is the order adjudging the minor a ward or committing him to the Youth Authority a sentence.[11]

In an earlier case, however, the statute was criticized.

> While the juvenile court law provides the adjudication of a minor to be a ward of the court shall not be deemed

[10]This summary is drawn from an unpublished paper written by M. Horiuchi, "Court Decisions Relating to Juveniles." Mr. Horiuchi is a graduate student in Police Administration at San Jose College and also a senior deputy probation officer with the Santa Clara County Juvenile Probation Department, San Jose, California.

[11]In re Johnson, 1966, 227 C.A. 2d 37, 38 Cal. Rptr. 405.

to be a conviction of a crime, nevertheless, for all practical purposes, this is legal fiction, presenting a challenge to credulity and violence to reason.[12]

The United States Supreme Court also indicated discomfort with the proceedings being held civil in a case referred from New York in 1970.

> In effect, the Court of Appeals distinguished the proceedings in question here from a criminal prosecution by use of what *Gault* called a "civil" label of convenience which has been attached to juvenile court proceedings. . . . We made clear in that decision that civil labels and good intentions do not themselves obviate the need for criminal due process safeguards in juvenile courts. . . .[13]

Arrests

Although the California Welfare and Institutions Code allows for the arrest of juveniles without a warrant, regardless of whether a misdemeanor or felony was committed in the officer's presence, an arrest must be lawful and based on more than hearsay.

> Police officers' testimony that defendant's name had appeared on a board at police headquarters after being named by various people in some undescribed way was not sufficient to justify defendant's arrest without a warrant. The legality of an arrest must be measured by information possessed by the arresting officer at the time of the arrest, and not by the total information gained later.[14]

Bail

Presently, juveniles undergoing delinquent proceedings are not generally considered eligible for bail. In California, bail has not been much of an issue, and the matter was resolved several years ago.

[12]*In re Contreras*, 1952, 109 Cal. App. 2d 787, 241 P. 2d 631.
[13]*In re Winship*, App., 1970, 38 L. W. 4253.
[14]*In re Rambeau*, 1968, 2666 Ac.A. 455, 72 Cal. Rptr. 171.

An order adjudging a person to a ward of the juvenile court is not a conviction of crime, and proceedings to have wardship declared are not criminal proceedings. It follows that the provisions relating to bail contained in Article I, Section 6 of the California Constitution and Section 1271 and 1272 of the Penal Code do not apply to such proceedings.[15]

However, when the court interprets the Constitution differently, bail has been granted.[16] In 1968, the U.S. Supreme Court considered bail as one of the issues and remanded the case back to the Ohio Court of Appeals for "reconsideration in light of Gault."[17] Bail, thus far, is a matter of state law and is provided for in nine states: Alabama, Arkansas, Colorado, Georgia, Massachusetts, Michigan, North Carolina, South Dakota, and West Virginia. The U.S. Supreme Court has not seen fit to make any changes in this area.

Moreover, tribunals of this nature were established with the view of showing more consideration to the juvenile and were not designed to deprive him of any of his constitutional rights. A finding of delinquency usually demonstrates the necessity for making a change in the custody of the child, but prior to such a finding, he is entitled to his constitutional right to bail.[18]

Right to Counsel

The matter of representation by counsel was made clear by the U.S. Supreme Court in the Kent decision of 1966.

The right to representation by counsel is not a grudging gesture to a ritualistic requirement. It is of the essence of justice. Appointment of counsel without according an opportunity for hearing on a "critically important" decision is tantamount to denial of counsel.[19]

[15]*In re Magnuson*, 1952, 110 C.A. 2d 73, 242 P. 2d 362.
[16]*State v. Franklin*, 1963, 202 La. 439, 12 So. 2d 211.
[17]*In re Whittington*, 1968, 391 U.S. 341, 20 L. Ed. 625, 88 S. Ct. 1507.
[18]18 Vand. L. Rev. 2096 (Oct. 1965).
[19]*Kent v United States*, 1966, 383 U.S. 541, 18 L. Ed. 527, 87S. Ct. 1045.

Since the Gault case in 1967, most states require that "Miranda warnings" be applicable to juveniles.[20] The Miranda Decision requires that certain legal requisites be fulfilled when an officer engages a suspect on the street and questions him. *The officer must advise the suspect of his right to remain silent; of his right to speak to an attorney; that if he wishes an attorney but cannot afford one, the State will provide him with one; and that anything the suspect says may be held against him.*

Jury Trial

Like bail, jury trial in juvenile proceedings is not granted in most states. A Nebraska case was declared unappropriate by the U.S. Supreme Court and the writ of per curiam was dismissed. One of the issues presented to the Court in this case included the right to a jury trial by juveniles.[21] California had two cases appealed on this subject. In the first case, the court stated:

> Juvenile court proceedings are not primarily criminal in nature; therefore, trial by jury is not a constitutional requirement.[22]

The second case made reference to the Gault decision.

> To adopt trial by jury in the juvenile court would "introduce a strong tone of criminality into the proceedings," destructive of the beneficial purposes of the juvenile court law, not warranted as a due process of law safeguard of individual rights.[23]

There are certain exceptions, since some states have statutes providing for jury trial. However, the juveniles must demand trial by jury, or the juvenile judge on his own motion must call for a jury trial.

[20]The decision by the U.S. Supreme Court made it explicitly clear that the *Miranda warnings* (i.e., advisement of rights) did apply to juveniles.

[21]*De Backer v. Brainard*, 1969, 90 S. Ct. 163, 38 L. W. 4001.

[22]*In re R. L.*, 1969, 83 Cal. Rptr. 81.

[23]*In re T. R. S.*, 1969, 1 Cal. App. 3d 178, 81 Cal. Rptr. 574.

The record discloses that counsel made no demand for a jury trial at the time of the hearing before the county court. It appears that the county court had jurisdiction of the person, jurisdiction of the subject matter, and jurisdiction to render the particular judgment which was rendered, and that the petition for habeas corpus should be denied.[24]

States that allow for jury upon demand in juvenile cases include Oklahoma, Texas, Tennessee, Nevada, and Georgia.

Self-Incrimination

The protection against self-incrimination applies to juveniles as well as to adults. No exceptions are noted. Even when confessions are obtained after advisement of legal rights, the questions of intelligent and voluntary waiver must be resolved prior to their use as admissible evidence in court.

The youth of the petitioner, the long detention, the failure to send for his parents, the failure immediately to bring him before the judge of the juvenile court, the failure to see to it that he had advice of a lawyer or a friend—all these combine to make us conclude that the formal confession on which this conviction may have rested was obtained in violation of due process.[25]

The 1967 Gault decision stated the youth's right against self-incrimination in a more direct and binding manner:

It would be entirely unrealistic to carve out of the Fifth Amendment all statements by juveniles on the ground that these cannot lead to "criminal" involvement. In the first place, juvenile proceedings to determine "delinquency," which may lead to commitment to a state institution, must be regarded as "criminal" for the purpose of the privilege against self-incrimination. We conclude that the constitutional privilege against self-incrimination is as applicable in the case of juveniles as it is with respect to adults.[26]

[24]*Ex parte Norris*, 1954, Okla. Crim. 268 P. 2d 302.
[25]*Gallegos v. State*, 1962, 370 U.S. 49, 8 L. Ed. 2d 325, 82 S. Ct. 1209.
[26]*In re Gault*, 1967, 387 U.S. 1, 18 L. Ed. 527, 87 S. Ct. 1428.

Double Jeopardy

As juvenile proceedings are still considered noncriminal and nonpenal, double jeopardy has yet to become an issue. In 1953, a California juvenile was certified back to the juvenile court after being confined for 15 months at the Preston School of Industry. He was then certified to an adult court from the juvenile court. Subsequently, he was committed to a state prison. Appeal was based on double jeopardy, but the court stated:

> It follows therefore that constitutional provisions against double jeopardy do not apply to this case, for the reason that the proceedings in the juvenile court was not a criminal prosecution.[27]

In a later case, a juvenile was remanded to an adult court after a preliminary hearing.

> Consequently, it was not improper for the juvenile court to conduct a hearing before determining whether or not to waive jurisdiction. To hold that jeopardy attached at that point would preclude the full and informal investigation in the interests of the minor and the community which Congress thought necessary to achieve the salutary remedial purposes of a juvenile court system.[28]

However, once a juvenile stands trial for an offense, and a disposition has been made for that specific offense, juvenile courts are reluctant to subject the juvenile to another trial. In *Garza* v. *State*, a judgment was reversed, and the prosecution was ordered to be dismissed.

> Conviction of defendant for murder violated principles of fundamental fairness and constituted a deprivation of due process where prior to such conviction, which occurred after defendant reached the age of 17 years, defendant upon petition of the district attorney, had been adjudged a delinquent child on basis of the same act of murder and had been held in custody as a delinquent child.[29]

[27] *People* v. *Silverstein*, 1953, 121 C.A. 2d 140, 262 P. 2d 656.
[28] *U. S.* v. *Dickerson*, 1959, 106 App. D.C. 211 F. 2d 487.
[29] *Garza* v. *State*, 1963, 369 S. W. 2d 36.

The quantum of proof required varies from state to state, and some states in the past have indicated that a preponderance of evidence was sufficient. However, the issue was resolved by the U.S. Supreme Court recently.

> We therefore hold, in agreement with Chief Judge Fuld in dissent in the Court of Appeals, "that, where a 12-year-old is charged with an act of stealing which renders him liable to confinement for as long as six years, then as a matter of due process . . . the case against him must be proved beyond a reasonable doubt."[30]

Due process as stated in the Fourteenth Amendment is now becoming applicable to the delinquent proceedings in juvenile courts. The law has been declared by the courts; and, when due process is ignored or circumvented, the juvenile courts are subject to sharp criticisms.

> There is evidence, in fact, that there may be grounds for concern that the child receives the worst of both worlds; that he gets neither the protections accorded to adults nor the solicitous care and regenerative treatment postulated for children.[31]

It was stated again in *Gault*:

> We do not mean . . . to indicate that the hearing to be held must conform with all of the requirements of a criminal trial or even of the usual administrative hearing; but we do hold that the hearing must measure up to the essentials of due process and fair treatment.[32]

The decisions by the U.S. Supreme Court and the state appellate courts have had a tremendous impact on the juvenile court system throughout the United States. What impact the new emphasis on children's rights can have on the courts is shown by Philadelphia County's experience.

There, the number of judges assigned to juvenile cases

[30]*In re Winship*, 1970, 38 L. W. 4253.
[31]*Kent v. United States*, 1966, 383 U.S. 541, 18 L. Ed. 84, 87 S. Ct. 1045.
[32]*In re Gault*, 1967, 387 U.S. 1, 18 L. Ed. 527, 87 S. Ct. 1428.

has risen from two to five in the past five years. A dozen lawyers are on call to defend accused delinquents—and, in such cases, the district attorney must be represented, too. While the total caseload has changed little in recent years, pre-courtroom settlements rose from 1,921 in 1966 to 2,533 in 1967. Institutional commitments, meanwhile, declined from 1,736 to 1,160. Philadelphia County has had to hire more probation officers to supervise the growing number of youngsters released in pre-courtroom conference.

Summary

Chapter 4 examines the purpose, functions, and operation of the juvenile court. The philosophy of the juvenile court, as expressed here, is that the state must step in and exercise guardianship over a child living under the adverse social or individual conditions which develop crime. Further, the juvenile court provides a plan whereby the child may not be treated as a criminal, or legally charged with a crime, but as a ward of the state, to receive virtually the same care, custody, and discipline that are accorded the neglected and dependent child. This care shall approximate as nearly as possible that which the child should be given by his parents. *Parens patriae*, a Latin phrase, best sums up the idea of the juvenile court. *Parens patriae* refers to the English concept of the king in the role of the parent—a theory accepted in the United States as a foundation of the juvenile court.

Historically, the juvenile court was introduced in 1899, in Cook County, Illinois. From the inception of the juvenile court, the idea was that children were not to be treated as criminals or dealt with by the process used for criminals.

The jurisdiction of the juvenile court is *equity jurisdiction* and, as such, it has five characteristics of equity jurisdiction:

1. It is relatively informal in its procedure.
2. It is remedial—not punitive.
3. It acts preventively in advance of any specific wrongdoing.
4. It employs administrative rather than adversary methods.
5. It is individualized justice.

The chapter points out that the structure of the juvenile court and its position or status in the state's organizational pattern varies among the different states and, on occasion, even within the particular state.

In conclusion, Chapter 4 focuses on referrals and procedural requirements. It reviews the "screening process" and presents a brief survey of recent court decisions that affect police services for juveniles.

Selected References

ELDEFONSO, E., *Law Enforcement and the Youthful Offender: Juvenile Procedures*, Chap. 2. New York: John Wiley & Sons, Inc., 1967.

GIBBONS, D. C., *Delinquent Behavior*, Chap. 3. Englewood Cliffs, N. J.: Prentice-Hall, Inc., 1970.

KETCHAM, O. W., "The Unfulfilled Promise of the Juvenile Court," *National Council on Crime and Delinquency*, 7, No. 2 (Apr. 1961), pp. 98–99.

O'CONNER, G., and N. A. WATSON, *Juvenile Delinquency and Youth Crime: The Police Role*, Chap. 4. Washington, D. C.: International Association of Chiefs of Police, 1964.

Task Force Report: Juvenile Delinquency and Youth Crime, The President's Commission on Law Enforcement and Administration of Justice, Chap. 1 and Appendices A, C, and D. Washington, D. C.: Government Printing Office, 1967.

Police
Services
for
Juveniles:
From
Arrest
to
Disposition

The primary responsibility of law enforcement is the control and prevention of crime and delinquency through the enforcement of laws defining conduct considered detrimental to the good order of society. Since many criminal acts are committed by minors under the age of 18 (see Chapter 2), a large proportion of police work involves the detection, investigation, apprehension, and referral of these juveniles. In addition, law enforcement agencies are concerned with minors who come to their attention for noncriminal reasons, such as incorrigible behavior, truancy, and lewd and immoral conduct.

Current statistics on police contacts with juveniles are impressive and indicate how important the police role is. Naturally, the extent of local police authority and responsibility and the manner in which local forces exercise them depend both on the particular powers given a local police force by law and as affected by judicial interpretation, and on the limitations provided by law. The attitude and policy of the department head may also have an effect to some degree. As a result of these variables, the number and types of functions carried out by the police department in one community may exceed or differ from those undertaken in another.

chapter
5

Although the variables, as mentioned above, do have a definite influence on the functions carried out by police departments in various communities, law enforcement officials have always been concerned with the control of juvenile crimes. However, within the past two decades, police organizations began placing particular emphasis on their work with juveniles, and a definite trend in the development of specialized juvenile police services has been established.

Specialization

While the growth of the delinquency program contributed to the increased emphasis on juvenile police work, other factors were probably equally responsible. The patrolman walking a beat 30 years ago had a greater opportunity to know intimately the inhabitants and social institutions in his area than does the patrolman today. He could also more easily resolve minor law-enforcement problems. Urbanization has complicated the patterns and problems of social existence, as O'Connor and Watson vividly point out:

> A nation on the move from the farm to the city—such is the United States. The technological and industrial facets of our economy have met to bring people into the crowd of centralized living. We have moved from a farm-based economy to a city-centered economy. The compression of persons into our urban centers has added to the complexity of our concern. . . . The density of population in our cities serves also to bring persons into conflict with increased frequency. . . . The phenomenon of juvenile delinquency and youthful criminality represent the end products of diverse, complex, and presently insoluble social and personal problems.[1]

As a result of this situation, police departments in many communities have either appointed and trained officers to specialize in work with children, or have set up special juvenile units, according to the size of the department. Such

[1]G. W. O'Connor and N. A. Watson, *Juvenile Delinquency and Youth Crime: The Police Role* (Washington, D. C.: International Association of Chiefs of Police, 1964), p. 16.

movement toward specialization for work with juveniles has, of course, produced its problems. Police executives have had to experiment and to evolve policies largely by trial and error. "Whether or not to assign officers to specialized duty in connection with juvenile cases, the extent and degree of specialization, and the duties and responsibilities of the specialists are important questions for police administrators. The decision to specialize is based upon the theory that a specialist, because of superior knowledge and more intimate acquaintance with the problems, can do a better job. In large, more complex communities, the need for specialization is generally considered to be more pressing. Specialization in large police departments is probably both essential and inevitable. There, the question is not whether to specialize, but, rather, just what added duties should the specialist assume and what should they take away from other personnel."[2]

Specialized juvenile units in police departments are known by various names in the United States. They are called, for example, crime prevention bureaus, youth aid bureaus, juvenile bureaus, juvenile divisions, and juvenile control bureaus.

The following are duties considered appropriate for juvenile control units:

1. Processing to disposition juvenile cases investigated by other units, with the possible exception of traffic cases.
2. Special patrolling of known juvenile hangouts where conditions harmful to the welfare of children are known or suspected.
3. Maintenance of records on juvenile cases.
4. Planning and coordinating a delinquency prevention program.

The question of a juvenile officer's responsibility for the investigation of offenses is a significant one in those departments big enough to allow for a great deal of specialization. Some such departments hold investigation by juvenile officers to a minimum, assigning cases to be cleared to an appropriate squad without reference to the age of the person thought to have committed the offense. In others, the juvenile control routinely investigates certain offenses connected with juven-

[2]*Ibid.*, p. 48.

iles. In this latter instance, a juvenile control unit might be given responsibility for investigating and processing to disposition specific cases such as:

1. Offenses concerning children and the family, including neglect, abuse, or abandonment.
2. Adults contributing to the delinquency of a minor; employing minors in injurious, immoral, or improper vocations or practices; and admitting minors to improper places.
3. Processing, possession, or sale of obscene literature when children are involved.
4. Bicycle thefts.
5. Offenses committed on school property.
6. Sex offenses involving juveniles, except forcible rape.
7. Gang warfare among juveniles.

It is particularly important for the juvenile control unit to have separate quarters in the police station. If possible, the outside entrance to these quarters should be located so that children and their parents can come and go without passing through other quarters in the building. But access to the other sections should be easy and convenient for the juvenile officers.

Maintenance of Records, Fingerprints, and Photographs

The utilization of records, fingerprints, and photographs in police work with juveniles often gives rise to controversy. It is not within the scope of this chapter to go into the differences of opinion about certain aspects of these subjects. Suffice it to say that records, fingerprints, and photographs are important police tools and should be maintained.

Records

Adequate records relating to children alleged or known to be delinquents should certainly be maintained by the police. There are several needs for such records:

1. To provide information—for the police themselves, the courts, and other interested agencies—on all police contacts, past and present, with a given juvenile.
2. To define delinquency areas.
3. To throw light on community conditions if they contribute to delinquency.
4. For use in evaluation of a delinquency prevention program.

The records that are maintained should be as brief as practicable and to the point. For example, a patrol officer's report form for taking a child into custody should cover all the facts needed but should be simple ana brief enough to ensure the officer's cooperative participation in the report system.

The main areas of controversy regarding police records on children relate to the kinds of cases to be recorded and who should have access to the records.

There is little question that records should be kept of all cases wherein a bona fide complaint is received, an investigation made, or a child taken into custody—in other words, on any case involving a child that requires action and disposition by the police.

Fingerprints and Photographs

Whether the police should fingerprint or photograph juveniles is a question that usually provokes much debate.

Some state laws forbid both fingerprinting and photographing of children except by order of the juvenile court. Elsewhere, the practice is determined by the policy of the police department; it varies from fingerprinting of all children taken into custody and suspected of an offense to fingerprinting of only those children suspected of serious offenses. Photographing is less widespread than fingerprinting, but practice follows a similar pattern.

Some people oppose fingerprinting juveniles on the grounds that this practice stigmatizes the youngster because it is associated in the public mind with criminal procedure. On the opposite side of the argument, many persons advocate the use of fingerprinting because it is the most accurate method of identification. In other words, it gives a complete record. The consensus of law enforcement personnel seems to be that the use of fingerprint records cannot be considered apart from the use of other types of records. Therefore, professionals in the field suggest that the same safeguards applying to other records of juveniles apply with special force to fingerprints, which are basically a form of record. Generally, it is agreed that:

1. No juvenile fingerprints should be recorded in a criminal section of any central fingerprint registry.
2. Because of the connotations associated with fingerprinting in the minds of many people, their use should be held to occasions where identification hinges upon evidence available only through their use and where sanctioned by law or juvenile court policies.
3. In many jurisdictions, the consent of the juvenile court must be obtained before such procedures are utilized.
4. Juvenile fingerprints should be destroyed after their purpose has been served.

These rules for the use and safeguarding of fingerprint records should also be applied to photographs. Further, the use of photographs should be authorized only when: (1) the juvenile has been taken into custody as the suspected or known committor of a serious offense such as robbery, rape, homicide, manslaughter, or burglary; (2) the juvenile has a long history of delinquency, involving numerous violations of the law, and there are reasonable grounds to assume that this pattern of behavior may continue; (3) the juvenile is a runaway and refuses to reveal his identity.

An important factor to be considered in the use of fingerprints and photographs is the need for positive identification, and this should be the major consideration in the development and implementation of a policy for fingerprinting. Thus, a person whose identity is verified by parents immediately after an arrest may not be printed unless there is evidentiary material for which comparison prints are needed. On the other hand, a youngster who has been caught in a burglary should be printed so that the latent prints from future and past burglary scenes may be compared against a single or complete file of known offenders. The organization of fingerprints in this fashion is considered by law enforcement agencies as a vital investigative aid, and the age of the burglar cannot reasonably be offered as the basis for using or excluding such a technique. The psychological and emotional trauma of the burglary itself is what really counts, rather than any shock supposedly associated with the arrest and ensuing identification procedures.

Rights of Juveniles

The indispensable precondition for the juvenile court to act in any case brought before it is the factual determination that the child or parent engaged in conduct specified in the law to impower court action. Concern for the child's welfare may powerfully lead to attempts to mold the adjudicatory process so as to avoid unnecessary harm to the child. However, one defect of the administration of juvenile justice is that concern has often been allowed to substantially interfere with the goals of fairness and reliability in the adjudicatory process.

There have been significant changes in juvenile court laws throughout the United States in recent years. Such changes have been attributed to the 1967 decision of the Supreme Court in the Gault case previously discussed in Chapter 4. The Gault case has influenced some courts to adopt criminal court procedures with prosecutors appearing in behalf of the state. The Constitutional rights extended to children appearing in juvenile court are worth reviewing and are laid down as follows:

1. To comply with due process requirements, notice must be given sufficiently in advance of scheduled court proceedings so that reasonable opportunity to prepare will be afforded, and it must set forth the alleged misconduct with particularity.
2. The child and his parents must be notified that the child has a right to be represented by counsel retained by them and that if they are unable to afford counsel, counsel will be appointed to represent the child.
3. The child has the right to confront and cross-examine witnesses who testify, and he has the right to remain silent—that is, to exercise "the Constitutional privilege against self-incrimination"—at the hearing. "After a valid confession, a determination of delinquency and an

order of commitment to a state institution cannot be sustained in the absence of sworn testimony subjected to the opportunity for cross-examination. . . ."[3]

Although the Supreme Court has also spoken out on other matters such as taking a child into custody, detention, interrogation, and statements made by the child in custody, the law of the case consists of the three holdings on (1) notice, (2) counsel, and (3) self-incrimination, described above.

Evidence

Perhaps the height of the juvenile court's procedural informality is its failure to differentiate clearly between the *adjudication hearing* whose purpose is to determine the truth of the allegations and the petition, and the *disposition proceeding* at which the juvenile's background is considered in connection with deciding what to do with him. In many juvenile courts, adjudication and disposition are part of the same proceeding or are separated only in the minority of cases in which the petition's allegations are at issue. Even where the two processes are dealt with separately, the social reports, containing material about the background and character that might make objective examination of the facts of the case difficult, are often given to the judge before adjudication.

To lessen the danger that information relevant only to *disposition* will color factual questions of involvement and jurisdictional basis of action, the Children's Bureau has for some time recommended bifurcating juvenile court hearings (separating jurisdictional and dispositional hearings) just as judicially in the trial of criminal cases there is a sharp division between trial on the issue of guilt and the sentencing determination. Use of such a procedure makes possible a controlled and relatively well focused inquiry into the facts of the alleged conduct of adjudication and more general and searching inquiry into facts bearing upon need for supervision and disposition. It thus reduces the danger that the limitations of the adjudicatory hearing will narrow the dispositional determination and assures that the information appropriate to the dis-

[3]*Gault v. Arizona*, 1967, 387, U.S. 1, 18 L. Ed. 527187 S. Ct. 1428.

positional hearing will not unduly enlarge the scope of the adjudicatory hearing. As a result, it seems that many juvenile courts are gradually restoring the various procedures and safeguards of the traditional criminal court hearing.

Sensitivity to rules of evidence, issues, and facts of the case are becoming more predominant in juvenile court hearings and the nonadversary atmosphere which once prevailed is quickly disappearing.

Due process for children has now been held to entitle them to such criminal procedural rights as the right to jury trial,[4] the right to suppress evidence seized in violation of the Fourth Amendment,[5] and the right not to be placed twice in jeopardy in the juvenile court.[6]

The procedures which a police agency follows in gathering evidence of an offense involving a juvenile should be identical with those used in the investigation of cases involving adult suspects. The degree of proof required is no less for juveniles than for adults; and every care must be exercised to assure the rights of the child as those rights serve to protect him from unwarranted treatment or correction.[7]

Admonishment

Other aspects of procedural due process have also received the recent attention of the courts. In 1963 the Supreme Court ruled on the appeal case of *Gideon* v. *Wainwright*. The effect of this ruling was that new trials could be demanded by anyone convicted of a crime without legal counsel. Moving closer to the functions of police, in 1964 a decision was handed down in the case of *Escobedo* v. *Illinois*. This decision, based on a 5 to 4 majority, stated the Constitutional right of an indigent to be provided with legal counsel at the time of police interrogation. In June 1966, again by a 5 to 4 majority, the court ruled on the case of *Miranda* v. *Arizona*. The "Miranda Decision" had the effect of providing legal counsel for persons suspected of crimes

[4]*Piland v. Clark County Juvenile Court*, Nev. 1969, 457 P. 2d 523.
[5]*Ciulla v. State*, Tex. Civ. App. 1968, 434 S.W. 2d 948.
[6]*Matter of Fonesca*, Kings Co. Sup. Ct. 1969, 299 N.Y.S. 2d 493.
[7]O'Connor and Watson, *Juvenile Delinquency and Youth Crime*, p. 54.

during police questioning. Since this ruling and the previous ones were made on the basis of "Constitutional rights," law enforcement found itself compelled to regard many traditional investigative methods as "unconstitutional."

The rulings in these cases have been applied to the juvenile court process to provide guidelines in each of the following situations:

1. When a police officer takes a youth into custody, does the officer have to advise the youth of his rights to remain silent and get legal counsel?
2. When a law enforcement officer is engaged in conversation with a youth on probation or parole, does the officer have to advise the youth of his rights?
3. Does a probation officer interviewing a youth already in custody at juvenile hall have to advise the youth of his rights?
4. Does a probation officer in the same situation have to advise a youth of his rights if that youth is under supervision as a ward of the court?
5. Can a minor contract to waive his rights?

As a result of the Escobedo decision, the courts handed down a ruling requiring police officers to admonish suspects at the time of arrest. The U.S. Supreme Court subsequently ruled that California's method of admonishing was best, and suggested that all states adopt similar procedures.

As previously stated, the Miranda decision requires that certain legal requisites be fulfilled when an officer engages a suspect on the street and questions him. The officer must advise the suspect of his right to *remain silent*; of his right to *speak to an attorney*; that if he wishes an attorney but cannot afford one, the *State* will provide him with one; and, that anything the suspect says may be held *against* him.

The question then arose as to the admonishing of 10 to 12-year-olds. Would a youth of that age be able to understand what he was waiving? Although the youth may not understand the consequences of his waiver, it is common practice to admonish him. The courts are of the opinion that it is within the jurisdiction of the court to determine whether the youth is fit to waive his rights or whether he has knowledge of what was involved.

Concerning the problem of admonishing during the conversation between a law enforcement officer and a suspect who is a minor, it is common practice to admonish the minor if the officer is trying to *discover* what part the youth played in an offense. However, if an officer is talking casually with a youth who spontaneously reveals his participation in an offense for which he is subsequently taken before the court, the officer need not have interrupted the conversation to admonish the youth. Any evidence revealed by a minor in that manner was felt to be acceptable in a court hearing for determination of jurisdiction *and* wardship.

A copy of the police report, which includes a record of the admonition, does not accompany the probation officer's report to the court. Is it necessary then for the probation officer also to admonish, since he is presenting his own report to the court? Technically, there is no need for the probation officer again to advise a youth of his rights. However, if a probation officer has any doubts that the youth has been admonished, or if he is questioning the youth with an eye toward obtaining a *confession*, the probation officer should definitely admonish the youth again. It is suggested, however, that the probation officer admonish a youth in any case to ensure the admission of all evidence and testimony in the determination of wardship and the acceptance of the recommended disposition. In most cases, it is a matter of policy that the juvenile probation officers are to admonish at all times.

The admonition of youths on probation does not differ significantly from the admonition of suspects. Usually, if a youth is on probation and commits a *law violation*, he should be admonished. However, if a youth on probation commits an offense which would fall in a category of pre-delinquency (truancy, beyond control activities, etc.), he need not be admonished. And, furthermore, all felony-type offense cases involving minors, whether court wards or not, would require an admonition.

In regard to the question of proper admonition through more than one day of questioning, after a change in the officer conducting the questioning of a suspect, or prior to obtaining a written statement, it is desirable to admonish immediately at the time of arrest, at the scene of the arrest if possible; to have a written record of the admonition in the police report; to admonish prior to any written statement made by the suspect; and to admonish the suspect again at the start of each new day of questioning. If a different officer should assume the questioning of a suspect, that officer should also admonish the suspect.

In summary:

1. You should admonish *all* youthful suspects, regardless of their age.
2. You need not interrupt, to admonish, any spontaneous conversation in which a youth reveals his participation in an offense.
3. If a youth is on probation and commits an offense that would fall under the classification of a law violation (Section 602 of the Welfare and Institutions Code of the State of California), he should be admonished. If he is involved in an offense which can be considered a "non-Penal Code" violation (Section 601 of the Welfare and Institutions Code of the State of California), he need not be admonished.
4. Each officer questioning the suspect should admonish him.

Arrest vs. Detention

The matter of detention poses critical problems for police officers, both as to *whether* the child should be detained and as to *where* he should be detained.

Detention should be utilized only when it is needed to protect the welfare of the juvenile, protect the community, or guarantee the appearance of a child and family in court. No child should be detained as punishment or simply for the convenience of authorities. Nor should a child be detained because he comes from a "bad home." Even though the home is "bad," it may be worse to subject the child to detention care.

There is considerable reason to believe that at present many children are being held in secured custody unnessarily. Numerous surveys conducted by the National Probation and Parole Association attest to this condition. Many children are placed in secured custody and subsequently released without ever being referred to the juvenile court. Of the children referred to the court, experience has shown that the majority of them can be safely allowed to remain in their homes pending juvenile court hearing.

The general lack of adequate facilities for the detention of delinquent children has long been an aggravating problem for the police. Where the community has no separate facility for the care and custody of delinquent children, it has been necessary to place the arrested youths in jail. Obviously, juveniles should not be held in jail. There is nothing in jail to contribute to their rehabilitation. A number of states have specifically forbidden or placed stringent restrictions on the use of jails for the detention of children. Yet, the fact remains that few communities provide separate detention facilities, and that in many communities lacking such facilities, there are occasionally children who need to be held in secured custody. What is the police officer to do in such a case? In the absence of any other solution than confinement in the jail, the police officer should see to it that the detention period is as brief as possible, that special care is given the child, and that the juvenile is quartered apart from adults in jail.

In those communities that possess a detention home and in which the police department has assigned special officers for work with children, the youngster who is to be detained should be conducted to the facility by a juvenile officer in an unmarked car if possible. The officer should also be aware of the fact that detention is a frightening experience to most children and he should therefore reassure the child and his family by describing the detention facility and the procedures that will be followed there.

Law enforcement personnel play a significant role in alleviating the crowded conditions in juvenile halls throughout the United States. Policemen inherit a great deal of discretionary authority as to the manner in which a juvenile offender is processed. Not every adult wrongdoer is brought to trial for his misconduct, nor is every juvenile offender put through the mill of official processing. It is impossible to determine how many potential subjects of formal legal action are eliminated from the system at an early point, but bits and pieces of information when put together portray a law enforcement and judicial system that uses, and appears to

Police Services for Juveniles: From Arrest to Disposition

value, substantial discretion, particularly in the initial stages of handling.

For various reasons and to different extents, every community is committed to informal handling. Statistics reveal how many juvenile offenders come into official contact with the police; they do not reveal the number of unofficial contacts on the street or in the station house. In cases of more than brief or casual contact, a trip to the station house for questioning by the arresting officer or juvenile specialist is usually required. The dispositions available to the police range from outright release, usually to the parents, to referral to the juvenile court. Court referral may mean citation, filing of a complaint, or physical removal of the child to detention awaiting formal action. Between those extremes are referral to community resources selected by the officer and station adjustment, by which is meant the juvenile's release on one or more conditions. Across the country, it is clear that discretionary action by the police in screening juvenile offenders accounts for the removal of significant numbers from juvenile halls and the formal juvenile justice system.

The conditions under which a child may be taken into custody are generally spelled out in a state's juvenile court law. Many state juvenile court laws contain the provision that "any child found violating any law or ordinance, or whose surroundings are such as to endanger his welfare, may be taken into custody without a warrant." This particular provision pertaining to apprehension without warrant as quoted from the Standard Juvenile Act is certainly broad enough to meet all practical contingencies.

Only a relatively small proportion of the total number of delinquent children with whom the police have contact need to be taken into custody. The majority of this group give the police no particular trouble other than concern for their welfare and where they can best be helped. But, there is a small group of adolescent delinquents—generally to be found in the upper-age limits of the juvenile court jurisdiction—whose behavior can give the police a great deal of trouble and make the process of taking them into custody a serious matter. Utmost care should be taken when placing this type of youngster into custody. Such a youngster can be considered quite dangerous due to his inability to control his impulses and inconsistencies in his reaction to stress.

Arrest vs. Detention

If a child is taken into custody, it should be the *duty of the police officer* to locate the parents, guardian, or custodian of the child as soon as possible thereafter. For this purpose, the child may be held by the police temporarily.

The officer then, whenever possible, should return the child to his parents, with a notice to the parents that the child's and their presence may be required by the juvenile probation department (citation). However, if the parents cannot be found within a reasonable period of time, or, if generally after consulting with the parents the officer is of the opinion that the interests of the child or the safety of the community warrant the child's detention, the officer should take the child to the place of detention or shelter designated by the court in accordance with agreed written procedures. Because arrest and disposition of neglected (dependent) and abused children may differ somewhat from the "routine" investigation of law violations, let us take a brief look at police services in this area.

The Police Role in Neglected and Abused Cases

Generally, the role of the police in cases of neglect can be broken down into receiving and investigating, verifying, evaluating, and disposing of complaints. In a previous book by the author,[8] the role of the police in the above area is covered as follows:

Receiving and Investigating Complaints: Situations involving neglect of children usually are brought to the attention of the police by someone other than the parents. Sometimes instances of neglect are observed by police while responding to other calls.

The officer should be certain to learn whether the present case of neglect is an isolated incident or whether it is part of a longtime pattern of neglect that would call for court action.

It may be necessary in some cases for the police officer

[8] E. Eldefonso, *Law Enforcement and the Youthful Offender: Juvenile Procedures* (New York: John Wiley, 1967).

to arrange for pictures to be taken within the home. Photographs will provide visual proof that undesirable conditions exist. Calling appropriate persons to witness such conditions is sometimes also advisable. In a case where cruelty on the part of a parent toward a child is indicated, a licensed physician should be asked to make a physical examination of the child so that he can testify in court about the child's condition.

Verifying Complaints: The initial question which should concern the police in responding to reported complaints of abuse or neglect of a child is: "Does neglect or abuse exist?" This fact should be established by a proficient police investigation, based on knowledge of the law and of the offenses governed by law, rules of evidence, and previous police experience in handling such complaints. Methods of gathering evidence include statements of witnesses and complainant, interviews with parents and children, and general observation.

Evaluating Complaints: After observing and investigating home conditions and discussing the case with the family and witnesses, an evaluation of the situation should be made by the police officer. This evaluation should include those aspects of the case regarded as legally and socially significant: the seriousness of the situation, the need for immediate protection of the child, observations concerning the physical conditions of the child, attitudes of parents, statements of witnesses, and general conditions of the home. This evaluation is not a social history, since it differs in purpose, scope, and degree, but is simply a process for arriving at police disposition.

Disposing of the Case: A number of cases can be closed by a warning or a reprimand. As mentioned before, in dealing with neglect situations it is important for the police officer to be aware of the many pressures that may cause parents to neglect their children. Rather than being willful, the neglect may simply be a symptom of the fact that these pressures have mounted beyond control. In such cases, the police officer may find it more suitable to refer the parents to a social agency for help. Through such means as good interviewing techniques, the police officer should try to differentiate between those who want to be and can be helped by a social agency, and those who have shown, by willful neglect of their children, that they need the authoritative service of the court.

A police officer should be informed about the community agencies that can be of service in neglect cases. Definite policies for referral should be arranged between the police and such agencies. Smoothly working relations with the agencies will enable the police department to explain their services to parents in need of referral.

Minor instances of neglect or misconduct by parents toward their children may most appropriately be dealt with by a reprimand regarding the matter and a warning of the possible consequences if the act is repeated. For example, a police officer may be dispatched in response to neighbors' reports that a child is being beaten. Upon investigating, the officer may find no conclusive evidence that the beating is beyond the normal discipline within parental prerogatives. However, if the facts warrant it, the officer may want to make it clear to the parents that under certain circumstances such an incident could lead to further action by the police in behalf of the child.

On the other hand, there are instances where the officer, before disposing of certain cases, should check the records of the police department and other community agencies to determine whether the family has been known previously. In any event, adequate records should be maintained regarding the complaint, normal facts of the investigation, and the police disposition.

Court action involving the neglect of children is called for when:

1. The alleged neglect constitutes an immediate danger to the health and welfare of the child and the facts on hand are sufficient to support a petition.
2. The alleged neglect does not constitute immediate danger to the health and welfare of the child, but there is reason to believe that court action or service is needed to protect or aid the child and the facts on hand are sufficient to support a petition.

If these conditions do not strictly apply, as previously mentioned, the police may first try other dispositions, if the department policy and agreement with the local courts permit such steps. Policies relative to court action against adults should be worked out jointly by the police department, the juvenile court, other courts that might be involved, and the prosecuting attorney's office.

Investigation of Juvenile Offenses[9]

All juvenile offenses should be as fairly and completely investigated as possible. Some police officers are said to show a tendency to neglect certain facts in the investigation of juvenile offenses on the *assumption* that the juvenile court does not need or require detailed facts and evidence. This assumption, as we have attempted to communicate, is incorrect. Full information concerning the case is always needed to sustain petitions.

The techniques used in the investigation of offenses should be those developed by police science, as taught in the best police academies and treated in standard texts on police investigation. Although a definitive treatment of these techniques is beyond the scope of this chapter, the highlights of investigating juvenile offenses will be discussed.

The specialized work of criminal investigation has two primary purposes:

(1) the gathering of facts and other information for examination to determine whether a criminal violation has been perpetrated and, if there is a violation, the identity of the violator; and

(2) the collection, preservation, and preparation of evidence that will be admissible and effective before a court or jury to convict a defendant standing trial for his actions.

In fulfilling these two purposes, the investigator must adhere to and be guided by Constitutional law. His evidence in a criminal case must be admissible in a court of law and must follow the basic rule for all investigators that evidence

[9]Portions of this section were adopted with permission of John Wiley & Sons, Inc. From E. Eldefonso, *Law Enforcement and The Youthful Offender: Juvenile Procedures* (New York: John Wiley, 1967), pp. 88–98.

secured against a defendant in the violation of his Constitutional rights will not be admitted into evidence.

The criminal investigator must be searching constantly for new and more refined methods of investigation, just as the crime community is never idle in devising new patterns of crime.[10]

It must be recognized that it is not the function of police officers to do casework, and that they do not make comprehensive case studies. The social information they do secure during the investigation of a juvenile crime must be limited to that needed for a general understanding of a youngster's situation so that he may be referred to the proper source for help.

There are many factors in addition to social ones that the police officer must consider in the full investigation of a case. The following lists some important factors which should be included in such an investigation:

1. Factors of the offense, including all details necessary to sustain a petition in court;
2. Record of any previous police action;
3. Record of any previous court or social agency action;
4. Attitudes of the child, his parents, and the complainant in the offense toward the act;
5. Adjustment of the child at home, in school, and in the community.

Any variety of methods is utilized by the police agencies in reporting the offenses to and communicating with the probation department. Generally, in delivering a minor to the probation department, it is incumbent upon the police officer to submit a cursory report, providing essential details, and follow up a day or two later with a full, written report. Some agencies send juvenile officers to complete the investigation and then report orally with a supplementary report to the investigating probation officer. Such information might include:

1. Facts of the offense, which gave the juvenile court jurisdiction over the case, and personal data about the juvenile;

[10]E. Eldefonso, A. Coffey, and R. C. Grace, *Principles of Law Enforcement* (New York: John Wiley, 1968), pp. 209–210.

2. Information about any co-delinquent or the complainant, including a statement regarding injuries or damages;
3. Any reasons for requesting juvenile court action other than, or in addition to, the specific offense;
4. A brief summary of any significant factors revealed in the investigation.

Every police officer has an obligation to familiarize himself thoroughly with the juvenile court philosophy and procedures so that he may interpret them to the child he refers to the court and the child's parents. The officer should avoid giving any suggestions as to what the probation department's study will lead to or what the court disposition may be, since these are matters outside his jurisdiction. However, there is no reason why the arresting officer should not insure the child and his family that the study made by the probation department will help the judge to make a disposition that will not be punitive but will be in the best interests of the child, his family, and the community.

*Guidelines for Police
Disposition*

After a police officer has made a thorough investigation of a delinquency case, he is ready to make a choice of disposition. The following are some of the ways in which he may dispose of the case.

Referral to the Juvenile Court: The criteria for referral to the juvenile court are as follows:

1. The particular offense committed by the child is of a serious nature.
2. The child is known or has in the past been known to the juvenile court.
3. The child has a record of repeated delinquency extending over a period of time.
4. The child and his parents have shown themselves unable or unwilling to cooperate with agencies of non-authoritative character.
5. Casework with the child by a non-authoritative agency has failed in the past.
6. Treatment services needed by the child can be obtained only through the court and the probation department.

7. The child denies the offense and the officer believes judicial determination is called for, and there is sufficient evidence to warrant referral, or the officer believes the child is in need of aid.

Release to Parents or Guardians without Referrals: Generally speaking, a delinquent's own home is the best place for him, whether he is referred to an agency in the community for treatment or not. Before releasing a child to his own home without other referral, however, a police officer should look for evidence of the parents' interest in the welfare of their child and of the family's ability to meet his problems. Certain criteria that might lead a police officer to select this disposition for a delinquent case are as follows:

1. The offense is minor in nature, and there is no apparent need for treatment.
2. The child shows no habitual delinquency pattern.
3. The family situation is stable.
4. The relationship between the child and his parents is good. The parents seem aware of the child's problems and able to cope with them.
5. Adequate help is being given by public or voluntary agencies in the community.

In actual practice, release to parents or guardians without referral is probably the disposition most frequently made by the police officers in delinquency cases. There is some question, however, as to whether this disposition should be used as often as it is. The release to parents or guardians might be more successful if the child and parents were referred to another agency in the community for help.

There are indications that police officers do not use non-authoritative treatment resources to the maximum advantage. It is true that in many communities such resources are either limited or nonexistent, but it seems likely that in many places these resources are not utilized more than they are because of the failure on the part of the police, the agencies, or both to work out a more cooperative and mutually helpful relationship.

The delinquent who would be an appropriate referral to a social agency is a child who is not referred to the juvenile court, but whose delinquency is sufficiently serious to demand professional attention that he cannot receive from his parents. This is a child whose misconduct is just beginning rather than one whose pattern of antisocial behavior is serious and well-established. In many cases, the family of such a juvenile might also be referred to an agency.

In order to make a referral to the appropriate agency, a police officer must know about the needs of the child and his family and also about their willingness to ask help of such treatment resources.

To prepare a child and his family for referral, the officer should do a constructive job of explaining the functions of the agency. He should describe the special skills of the workers employed in the agency and how they are able to help the children and parents with specific problems. The officer should make it clear that problems can be solved only through the joint efforts of the agency and the child or his parents and that the agency cannot undertake to help them without their active interest and participation.

The officer should also provide specific information as to the name and address of the agency, the telephone number, and the person to contact: Agency referrals can be made in any of a number of ways:

1. By the police themselves, either by individual officers, or by a special referral unit.
2. Through the intake division of the probation department of the juvenile court.
3. By an information and referral division of the community welfare council or council of social agencies. In some communities, this referral unit is a case conference committee of the council.

Interviews and Interrogations

The interview, broadly defined, is used in every stage of the criminal process and is probably the most important means that the police officer has for carrying out his investigation. While conducting an investigation, the officer may also make extensive use of interrogation. The reputation of the department, as well as the effectiveness of the police officer's work, may depend on how well he uses both of these techniques. Although interviewing and interrogation appear to be similar, there are some basic differences between them.

An *interview* is a serious conference or conversation between two or more persons with the definite purpose of either obtaining certain information from the person interviewed about himself or another person, or effecting a change in his behavior or attitudes. It differs from ordinary conversation in that it has the purpose of influencing another person in a planned direction, whether it be that of making him willing to give information or to change his conduct. Ideas are exchanged not only through words, however. The skilled interviewer also relies upon his observation of gestures, tone of voice, inflections of speech, facial expression, and all the other means of expression used by human beings, consciously or subconsciously.

It may be concluded readily that the process of interviewing as defined covers a large area and could include that of speaking with suspicious persons on the streets, talking with witnesses to gain information and clear understanding regarding a particular offense or investigation, or obtaining information with reference to the background of police applicants, criminal suspects, informants, or any number of persons. Through the process known as *interviewing*, the police officer and investigator will learn a great deal of information and facts which are of extreme importance to him if he is to fulfill his assignments in a forthright manner.[11]

The following are basic to police interviewing:

Listening is better than talking. The police officer will not learn much if he does all the talking.

Play a "waiting game." Sometimes a person will "give," sometimes he will not. Information—that is, significant information—cannot be forced out of the interviewee. While it is true that the police officer is usually pressed for time, the interview situation must be cultivated in such a way as to allow the subject to express himself. Permit him to talk at his own speed. Questions should be for the purpose of directing the subject's conversation into productive channels.

[11]E. Eldefonso, A. Coffey, and R. C. Grace, *Principles of Law Enforcement*, p. 215.

The location of the interview is important. Privacy is a necessity. If there are telephones or other distractions, the subject will not feel at ease and will resist.

Asking questions and writing down the answers verbatim is not interviewing. If this were so, a tape recorder would do a better job. The interviewer should apply himself completely to the interview, then write down notes immediately afterward.

Two is company; more, a crowd in an interview. Generally, only one person should be in an interview at a time. Exceptions occur (where a family conference is conducted, for example), but usually the purpose of an interview will be defeated if more than the interviewer and the subject are present. If the youngster is to be interviewed, the parents can be cordially excused and what has been discussed can be presented to them later.

"Who does what?" should be made clear. The interviewer should explain who and what he is, what his purposes are, and where he stands in relation to the subject. Doubts, surmise, and suspicion negate an interview.

To understand the subject, it is necessary, when possible, to *see things from his point of view.* The police officer must avoid "talking down" to him. And the interviewer should use language the interviewee can understand. Much valuable information can be gathered by correspondence and telephone; however, personal interviews are basic in securing the kind of information and insight which are necessary for preparing an adequate report.

The aim of the police officer in the interview is to learn as much as possible about the facts of the offense and, when appropriate, about the child who is believed to have committed the offense, all knowledge that will help him to dispose of the case in the best interests of the community and the child.

In contrast, *interrogation* may be defined as:

The questioning of a person who is suspected of, has confessed to, or in fact has committed a crime or public offense. *Interrogation is an art,* and competent interrogators are rare in the police profession. Much skill, experience, and training are necessary before a person is considered a master at interrogation.

Interviews and Interrogations

The one factor that distinguishes the interrogation from the interview is the atmosphere in which each is conducted. The atmosphere of the interview is usually more relaxed and the person is more likely to "open up" and supply the desired information. . . . On the other hand, an interrogation usually is conducted with a person who is reluctant, for any number of reasons, to converse with a law enforcement officer. The atmosphere and tenor of the conversation is not as relaxed as in the interview, and the success or failure of the interrogation depends in large part, as stated before, on the skill and ability of the interrogator to develop the hidden knowledge or information possessed by the person being interrogated.[12]

Recently, the U.S. Supreme Court has placed several restrictions on the police in this vitally important area of interviewing and interrogating. These restrictions have already been discussed at the beginning of this chapter and in Chapter 4, and, therefore, will not be repeated here. But, whether they are a safeguard against the overzealousness of police charged by some, or a well-meaning but unrealistic erosion of necessary police authority, is still a moot question. The practical result is the serious curtailment of the effectiveness of interrogation and interviewing as a police technique in many cases, especially when suspects are, in fact, guilty and have learned to rely on these restrictions for protection from punishment. In more cases than not, the police cannot prove guilt through physical evidence, such as fingerprints or witnesses, simply because there is none. Under these circumstances, it is necessary to question the suspect and to check out his statements. His alibi or any discrepancies in his answers may be the only source of proof of guilt short of his confession. If he cannot be interviewed or interrogated adequately, even this source of proof is cut off. Moreover, if he is innocent, he is denied an opportunity to prove it without being formally charged.

The police officer must be aware of the present emphasis of the courts on statements and confessions. Formerly, the pertinent question was: "Is the confession true?" but today the emphasis seems to be whether or not the statement, admission, or confession is free, voluntary, without coercion of any kind, and is made in the full and complete aware-

[12] *Ibid.*

ness and understanding of all the defendant's Constitutional rights. This emphasis by the courts in interpreting the *Fourth, Fifth, and Fourteenth Amendments* to the *U. S. Constitution* places very severe restrictions on the investigator. Many previously tried and proven techniques of investigators are no longer of any value or use. Today's police investigator must develop and use new techniques which for the present are acceptable to the courts.[13]

There are certain attitudes and types of behavior which every police officer should avoid in interviewing and interrogating, since they destroy respect for law enforcement and accomplish no good whatsoever. These can be listed as follows:

1. Using profanity or obscenity.
2. Branding children with such epithets as "thief," "liar," or "tramp."
3. Losing the temper.
4. Telling falsehoods.
5. Using physical force.
6. Making promises that cannot be kept.

One final recommendation must be made regarding interviewing and interrogation. Whenever possible, and especially in the case of children under the age of 13, the interview or interrogation should take place in the presence of the parents or guardians of the minor in order to protect the rights and best interests of the child. In most cases this is possible except when the presence of the parents or guardians would tend to interfere with the officer's duty to obtain the facts surrounding the alleged offense, or where the parents or guardians have themselves participated in (dependent, neglected, or abused children), or contributed to, the conduct of the minor being investigated. There may well be instances in which the presence of the parents will tend to block or impede investigation; in such a case, the officer may refuse them the right to be present at the interview. The officer, however, must always remember that he may be charged with having obtained a statement from the minor by means of duress or by the infringement of the minor's guaranteed rights.

[13]E. Eldefonso, A. Coffey, and R. C. Grace, *Principles of Law Enforcement*, p. 216.

Summary

As a result of the technological and industrial developments in our society (i.e., centralized living, compression of persons into urban centers, and the movement from a farm-based economy to a city-centered economy), police departments have set up special juvenile units and are training officers to specialize in work with children. The decision to specialize is based upon the theory that a specialist, because of superior knowledge and more intimate acquaintance with the problems, can do a better job than a generalist. Needless to say, specialization has produced problems—this chapter discusses some of them.

The chapter then examines the functions considered appropriate for juvenile control units, namely: (1) Processing to disposition juvenile cases investigated by other units, with the possible exception of traffic cases; (2) special patrolling of known juvenile hangouts where conditions harmful to the welfare of children are known or suspected; (3) maintenance of records on juvenile cases; and (4) planning and coordinating a delinquency program.

The utilization and maintenance of records, fingerprints, and photographs—important tools for police work with juveniles—are discussed. Although there is a great deal of debate regarding the manner in which these tools are used and maintained, there is no doubt that when they are used intelligently, such controversy is limited.

The chapter also discusses the *rights of juveniles* and the influence of the Gault case; the sensitivity in the juvenile court pertaining to rules of *evidence, issues,* and *facts* of the case and its predominance in juvenile court hearings; the *admonishing* of juvenile offenders (i.e., right to remain silent, right to speak to an attorney, provisions for the state to provide an attorney, and warning that anything the suspect says may be held against him); the matter of *detention*—when to detain and when *not* to—as well as police responsibilities in this area; *investigation* of juvenile offenses and *guidelines* for police disposition. In conclusion, methods of interviewing and interrogation are presented, and the officer is cautioned against using certain basic attitudes and types of behavior.

Selected References

INBAU, F., and J. E. REID, *Criminal Interrogation and Confessions*, Chaps. 1–3. Baltimore: Williams & Wilkins, 1962.

O'CONNOR, G. W., and N. A. WATSON, *Juvenile Delinquency and Youth Crime: The Police Role*, Chap. 5. Washington, D. C.: International Association of Chiefs of Police, 1964.

SCHILDER, C. L., "Juvenile Offenders Should Be Fingerprinted," *Federal Probation*, 11, No. 1 (Jan.-March 1947), 46–47.

The Southwestern Law Enforcement Institute (ed.), *Law Enforcement and the Juvenile Offender*, pp. 68–79. Springfield, Ill.: Charles C Thomas, 1963.

Task Force Report: Juvenile Delinquency and Youth Crime, The President's Commission on Law Enforcement and Administration of Justice, pp. 19–21. Washington, D. C.: Government Printing Office, 1967.

WINTERS, J. E., "The Role of the Police in Prevention and Control of Delinquency," *Federal Probation*, 21, No. 2 (June 1957), 3–6.

A Special Problem: Drug Abuse— The Youthful Scene

In the past few decades, law enforcement has become an increasingly complex and skilled profession demanding specialized knowledge in many fields. One of these fields is that of drugs and their abuse. Recent medical advances have brought many new drugs into being and some of them, while invaluable to the practice of medicine, can be abused.

The abuse of drugs is not a new problem for police. The criminal investigation files of our large cities provide ample evidence that thousands of Americans are seeking relief from stress and escape from reality with the aid of opium, morphine, heroin, cocaine, marihuana, codeine, meperidine, and "over-the-counter" and prescription sedatives. These drugs are subject to special laws and regulations. In addition, a number of non-narcotic drugs are being abused. *Stimulants* (like the amphetamine drugs) and *depressants* (like the barbiturates) head the list. Certain tranquilizers are also increasingly used for nonmedical purposes. And abuse of the hallucinogenic agents—LSD-25, mescaline, and psilocybin— has received considerable publicity.

chapter

6

Historical Perspective

Drug abuse is probably as old as the earliest civilizations. Man has used great ingenuity in identifying substances which ease tensions, although for centuries available agents remained relatively static, limited to botanicals and their derivatives. *Amphetamine* and *methamphetamine*, the main stimulant drugs used today, were synthesized in the 1920s as part of the search for a substitute for ephedrine. The first clinical use of amphetamine was in 1930, and it became apparent that the amphetamines were effective in retarding fatigue-induced deterioration in psychomotor performance and that, under medical supervision, they had some appropriate use for persons required to do routine tasks for prolonged periods under adverse circumstances.

The first barbiturate, Veronal, was introduced in 1903, and a large number of others followed in quick succession. The short-acting barbiturates, especially pentobarbital and amobarbital, came into widespread use within the last 20 to 30 years.

Amphetamine and barbiturate-type drugs were in widespread use before their dependence-producing properties were recognized. However, the eventual discovery of their ability to cause euphoria, dysphoria, and psychic stimulation did not lead to the removal of these drugs from over-the-counter nasal inhalers. Moreover, restricting the legal acquisition of stimulants to prescription medications did not put an end to their misuse or abuse; today, these drugs are part of a major medical and social problem.

As early as 1200 B.C. the hemp plant, *Cannabis sativa*, was described as a source of long textile fibers, and its "narcotic" properties were documented in Chinese writings by 200 A.D.

> It was first used for such commercial purposes as the production of rope and textiles. It is mentioned in ancient Sanskrit literature dating from 2000–1400 B.C. Later it was utilized for medicinal and anesthetic purposes by Chinese, Hindu, and Arab physicians. Not until the tenth century of the Christian era was it extensively used for intoxicant and euphoric properties in India and the Arabic countries. The peoples of Europe were familiarized with

Historical Perspective

the drug through the writings of various romanticists during the nineteenth century.[1]

Its numerous derivatives, which can be smoked, eaten, or drunk, have become known throughout the world by a variety of names, including hashish, bhang, ganja, dagga, and *marihuana* (sometimes spelled marijuana). Traffic in and use of cannabis derivatives now is restricted in virtually every civilized country in the world, including those where custom has allowed its introduction into religious rites.

Lysergic acid diethylamide (LSD) was synthesized in 1938, but it was not until five years later, when the drug was accidentally ingested in an infinitesimal amount, that its hallucinogenic properties were discovered. Subsequently, LSD was used by several investigators to induce a "model psychosis" thought to resemble schizophrenia. It was soon recognized, however, that the vivid hallucinations, spectacular illusions, and sensory distortions induced were not characteristic of that disorder, even though the resulting depersonalization was somewhat similar.

By the early 1960s, an increasing number of persons were abusing (self-administering) LSD. Its use may have been abetted by the publications of Aldous Huxley and Timothy Leary and his associates, lauding its "consciousness expanding" qualities. By 1965, the medical literature contained numerous reports of the adverse, and often catastrophic, effects of the drug, particularly among those with pre-existing severe psychopathological conditions. Twenty-seven patients with severe complications of self-administration of LSD were admitted to New York's Bellevue Hospital in a four-month period in 1965. Substantial numbers have since been admitted to that and other hospitals for the same abuse.

Today, LSD is recommended for only strictly controlled research, and its legitimate production and distribution are limited to research purposes by the Food and Drug Administration.

The cultivation of the opium poppy for its seed dates back to prehistoric times, probably originating in Mesopotamia. The ancient Egyptians and Persians, and later the Greeks and Romans, used opium extensively for medicinal

[1] D. P. Ausubel, *Drug Addiction: Physiological, Psychological, and Sociological Aspects* (New York: Random House, 1958), p. 95.

purposes and sometimes for pleasure-seeking purposes. Among Greek, Roman, and Arabic physicians, opium enjoyed the reputation of a fantasia and was enthusiastically prescribed for all ailments ranging from headache to leprosy. From the Mediterranean area, it was carried to India and China by Arabian traders. The opium poppy is now grown mainly in India, China, Turkey, Iran, and Yugoslavia. *Heroin* is the indirect derivative of the drug opium.[2]

> More than in the case of any other nations, opium has played a crucial and disastrous role in the history of China over the past 200 years. In addition to retarding economic development, opium cultivation and opium profits have corrupted political life and financed civil disorder and revolution.[3]

In recent years, the smoking of opium has virtually disappeared. This disappearance was probably brought about by the difficulties encountered in smoking without detection. Considerable paraphernalia and advance preparations are required before the smoking may commence. Once the pipe is lit, the opium gives off a distinctive, easily identified odor which will carry for a considerable distance and greatly increase the chances for detection.

Youthful World of Drugs

Many thousands of Americans are addicted or habituated to narcotics and other kinds of drugs. In New York City alone, there are an estimated 25,000 addicts.[4] It has been calculated that these 25,000 addicts must raise from $500,000 to $700,000 per day to support their habit. To raise the money needed, many turn to crimes such as robbery, shoplifting, burglary, forgery, and prostitution. Although less severe than in New York, the picture is comparable in Chicago, Los Angeles, Detroit, and other major cities throughout the country. Moreover, most qualified observers agree that the total consumption of drugs is increasing (Figure 6–1a and b).

[2]*Ibid.*, p. 57.
[3]*Ibid.*
[4]*Newsweek*, Feb. 16, 1970, p. 66.

Fig. 6.1a. The evidence of underground drug traffic reveals a steady increase of illegal drugs. Various drugs are confiscated at border stations throughout the United States. This photo, courtesy of the Ambassador College Research Department, vividly portrays the extent of the illegal drug traffic.

Fig. 6.1b. Officers of the San Jose, California, police department with a supply of drugs picked up during the arrest of 38 young suppliers. The officers worked as undercover operators in arranging many of the buys. On the table are 10,000 reds, hundreds of bennies, plus LSD, speed, and a gun seized from one suspect. Courtesy of *Campus Life Magazine*.

A national survey of college students completed in December 1970 by George Gallup revealed that the number of students who have tried marihuana and LSD had grown at a remarkable rate over a five-year period. Forty-two percent of the students surveyed stated that they had tried marihuana. This figure—42 percent—is almost double the figure obtained in a 1969 survey (22 percent) and is eight times as high as the 5 percent recorded in 1967.

According to the survey, the use of other drugs has also increased. Use of LSD jumped from 1 percent in 1969 to 14 percent in 1970. Use of barbiturates rose from 10 percent in 1969 to 14 percent in 1970, and use of amphetamines increased by 16 percent in the same one-year period. Marihuana continued to dominate the drug scene on campus (an example of experimentation on the college level along with attendance at rock festivals and participation in antiwar demonstrations, as graphically pointed out in many sources—see Figure 6–2). Of the total population sampled for survey,

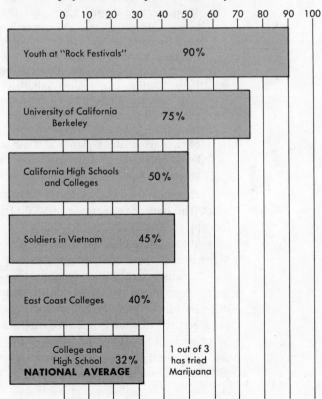

Fig. 6.2.
Percent of young people experimenting with marijuana.
Courtesy of the Ambassador College Research Department.

Youthful World of Drugs

more than a fourth (28 percent) indicated that they had used the drug. Approximately one student in six reported that he used it an average of four times a week over the 30-day period prior to Gallup's survey.

The drug situation in high schools is as upsetting as that in colleges:

> The drug revolution, barely begun on college campuses a few years ago, has already swept the nation's high schools. The use of drugs, particularly marihuana, is now an accepted fact of life from anywhere from 30 to 50 percent of all U. S. secondary-school students. "I'd compare buying dope today," says Eric Nelson, one of the brightest seniors at Newton (Mass.) High School, "with buying the school newspaper."
>
> Last month, surveys by both high school students and administrators pointed out just how widespread drug use really is. At Greenwich (Conn.) High School, the student newspaper took a sample of homeroom classes and reported that 46 percent of all seniors had smoked marihuana, 10 percent had tried LSD, and three percent had used heroin. "We do it," said a Greenwich senior who has already been accepted at the University of Connecticut, "because it's here, because we like it, and because it's one way to tell the grown-up world to go to hell." In Gross Pointe Park, Michigan, a wealthy suburb of Detroit, school officials surveyed 2,650 students from the fifth through twelfth grades, and ended up with similar findings. About half the seniors had used drugs at least once; frequent users often start in the eighth and ninth grades, and most students obtain drugs from friends without spending money and usually get them in their own or friends' homes.[5]

Although marihuana is the favorite student drug (at $20.00 an ounce, an increase of $8.00 from last year, enough for approximately 25 to 30 joints, or cigarettes), students also utilize Mescaline (a form of peyote), speed (usually Methedrine), and LSD. Stimulants and depressants—"ups" and "downs"—are also popular in high schools. The stimulants—amphetamines (diet pills, Dexedrine, and Benzedrine)—induce great bursts of energy and, quite frequently, are ingested before strenuous activities, such as sporting events or examinations. However, when these stimulants wear off, the user often has a difficult time. Therefore, a depressant pill—a barbiturate—is utilized. The "downs" include Seconal

[5] *Ibid.*

A Special Problem: Drug Abuse—The Youthful Scene

Fig. 6.3. San Jose City police detectives take inventory of $35,000 worth of marijuana and dangerous drugs found in the automobile trunk of a seventeen-year-old suspect arrested by the two officers. Courtesy of Gordon McLean, Executive Director, Santa Clara Valley Youth for Christ.

(reds) and Tuinal (blue and orange), both of which produce euphoria—an abnormal state of well-being and contentment not warranted by an individual's actual circumstances. Because the "ups" and "downs" are only ten to fifteen cents each, the average student has no difficulty in acquiring money for his supply.

Heroin, which causes powerful addiction, long considered the affliction of the criminal, the derelict, and debauched, is increasingly attacking America's children. Dr.

Youthful World of Drugs

Michael M. Baden, New York's Deputy Chief Medical Examiner, states that heroin use is now the leading cause of deaths among teenagers in New York City, where drug addiction has become a major public health problem apart from its extensive criminal aspects. Amplifying on drug addiction in New York, Dr. Baden reports that hepatitis, tetanus, endocarditis, bacterial infection of the heart, homicide, and suicide, are in high incidence among the heroin-user population. He further states that deaths among teen-agers, which constituted only 4 percent of the total deaths from heroin usage in 1918, now constitute 25 percent of the total, with the sharpest rises having occurred since 1967.[6]

> Part of the dread in the danger of the problem is that it spreads all too invisibly. No one knows how many heroin addicts of any age there are in the U. S. But in New York City alone, where most experts think half the heroin users in the U. S. live, 224 teenagers died from overdoses of heroin related infections last year, about a quarter of the city's 900 deaths from heroin use. So far this year, over 40 teenagers have died because of heroin. There may be as many as 25,000 young addicts in New York City, and one expert fears the number may mushroom fantastically to 100,000 this summer. Cautious federal officials believe that heroin addiction below age 25 jumped 40 percent from 1968 to 1969. However imprecise the figure is, there is no doubt in the magnitude of the change, or the certitude that something frightening is sweeping into the corridors of U. S. schools and onto the pavements of America's playgrounds. It has not yet cropped up everywhere, but many experts believe that disaster looms large.[7]

The problem is by no means limited to the schools, of course, but as previously stated, a large number of these addicts are of high school age. Some are even younger. They will live short, empty lives with neither hope nor meaning. They no longer have a choice.

Most of the serious drug problems exist in the heart of the major cities where there are too many people, too little money, and too little to do. However, drug abusers are found everywhere, from the worst slum areas to the wealthiest suburbs.

[6]*Time,* March 16, 1970, p. 16.
[7]*Ibid.*

A Special Problem: Drug Abuse—The Youthful Scene

The common factor underlying drug abuse is the attempt to escape from either physical or emotional problems. Young people are particularly vulnerable. Usually, they are introduced to drugs by friends, not by "pushers." It is hard to resist a group when you're the only holdout. It is a well-known fact that gangs and even otherwise amiable social groups are often responsible for the introduction of illegal drugs.

The figures mentioned are alarming, but they do not begin to reflect the real cost of the abuse of narcotics and certain other drugs. Thousands of drug abusers live for years in the shadows of society—only half alive, only half free.

Why Drugs?

To cope intelligently with drug problems, one needs to understand what kinds of appeals drugs offer. While people abuse them for a number of reasons, the most basic reason is that the individual involved lacks an adequate personality and fails to identify with adult goals. Because of his inability to formulate some type of identification with mature goals, such a person finds drugs useful in achieving two adjustive objectives: (1) *creating a pleasure-seeking structured environment for himself in which he can pursue effortless pleasurable activities; and* (2) *eliminating the intrusive demands and responsibilities associated with adult personality status. Such a person afflicted with a crippling personality turns to drugs because they help him realize his hedonistic objectives.*[8]

> After he takes his first few shots, the addict literally exclaims, "Boy, this is what I have been looking for all my life. What could be easier?" By merely injecting a needle under his skin, he satisfies his quest for immediate and effortless pleasure. Apart from the voluptuous thrill of the "kick," he reports increased self-confidence and feelings of self-esteem, decreased anxiety, and grandiose illusions (of wealth, power and omnipotence). Primary needs such as hunger and sex urges fade into the background and, although not directly gratified, are rendered so uninsistent as to be incapable of generating anxiety or frustration when their satisfaction is threatened or denied. Fear of pain is also

[8]D. P. Ausubel, *Drug Addiction*, p. 44.

set aside as the threshold for pain perception is raised and as its anxiety-producing implications are minimized. In fact, because of the drug's specific inhibition of the self-critical faculty, the environment in general assumes a more benevolent and less threatening aspect.[9]

In surveying the available literature on drug abuse, it is evident that there are many other explanations and ideas concerning the etiology of drug usage. Various disciplines (psychology, physiology, sociology, etc.) have contributed to literature on drug abuse. Moreover, many kinds of drug users are delineated, and the causes leading to use are thought to be multiple and frequently interrelated. However, all of the disciplines appear to concentrate on inadequacies of the user's personality. David P. Ausubel, a noted author and expert on drug abuse, concludes that:

> Differential susceptibility to drug addiction is primarily a reflection of the relative adjustive value which narcotics possess for different individuals. At any given moment, a person exposed to narcotics will only become an addict if the drug is able to do something significant for him psychologically, that is, to satisfy certain of his currently important needs.[10]

Perhaps the most definitive analysis of drug abuse among adolescents is Isador Chein's *The Road to H*.[11] Chein agrees with Ausubel's hypothesis that drug susceptibility is associated with the *adjustive* value of using drugs and concludes that:

> The evidence indicates that all addicts suffer from deep-rooted major personality disorders. Although psychiatric diagnoses are apt to vary, a particular set of symptoms seems to be common to most juvenile addicts. They are not able to enter into prolonged, close, friendly relations with either peers or adults; they have difficulties in assuming a masculine role; they are frequently overcome by a sense of futility, expectations of failure, and general depression; they are easily frustrated and made anxious, and they find frustration and anxiety intolerable.[12]

[9]*Ibid.*, pp. 44—45.
[10]D. P. Ausubel, "Causes and Types of Drug Addiction," *Key Issues*, Vol. 1 (Nov. 1961), 12.
[11]I. Chein, *et al.*, *The Road to H* (New York: Basic Books, Inc., 1964).
[12]*Ibid.*, p. 14.

In recent years, drug abuse has moved from city ghettos into the larger community, to middle-class and upper-middle-class neighborhoods and suburbs. Many adults and young people in these more affluent areas, like their less fortunate fellows, have found in drugs an answer to their problems and frustrations—a new excitement and an escape from boredom. Drug abuse initially offers them, as it does to others, a temporary sense of satisfaction and euphoria. Then the drugs proceed to destroy their hosts.

The high school student most likely to use drugs, according to a number of high school principals, deans, and suburban psychiatrists, is the bright student who does not participate in school activities, who often has a troubled home life, and who feels alienated from society. A recent interview conducted by Norman Melnick, staff writer for the *San Francisco Examiner*, with several Hillsborough (an upper-class suburban area on the outskirts of San Francisco) teen-agers, presents a good example of alienated youth. These youngsters were interviewed in a railroad station across from their school. According to Melnick, they were from well-off, some wealthy, families. They painted a vivid picture of the situation:

> Everybody says Hillsborough kids should wear velvet suits and lace shirts. I wanted to go around with greasy jeans and a big hole in my shirt—in the stomach. And I want to take drugs.
> Parents are after you all the time—they want to know everything you do. They want to follow you out of the door and they want to follow you home. They're snoopy. That's what we want to do, we just want to BREAK out. . . . All agreed (particularly a youth in a cowboy hat) that if they wanted some stuff right now, they could get it two minutes from here. One particular youth indicated that he had blown it in the kitchen of his place, gone back to school and freaked-out the rest of the day.[13]

An interview with a young adult, also conducted by Melnick, adds greater significance to the interview with the teen-agers.

[13]N. Melnick, Staff Writer, *San Francisco Examiner*, San Francisco, Calif., n.d.

Robert S., 23, has been on the road a lot: Mexico, New Orleans, Chicago, Boston, New York, and now San Francisco. Five years ago, he left home "because my parents seemed dead to me." His father is a Methodist minister from Pittsburgh, Pennsylvania.

Robert, who is beardless, shares an apartment with four other Haight-Ashbury hippies. The arrangement is called a commune. The first thing Robert usually does in the morning is listen to a Beatles' record. Then he dresses and heads for Tracy's, a coffeehouse.

Before noon, he appears at the "Free Frame of Reference," the Frederick Street headquarters of the "diggers," derived from seventeenth century England when little people united behind the idea of equal rights and property and were driven underground by Cromwell.

Haight-Ashbury "diggers" collect food, clothes, and money to lavish on other hippies. As a "digger," Robert does his chores in the afternoon and also spends some time dancing and walking on Haight Street, "where I might get stopped by a cop who asks me to move along or some silly thing." He's asleep at three in the morning.

What does he do evenings? After a long pause, Robert answered, "Make love." Robert uses drugs—LSD, marihuana, hashish (a more potent form of marihuana). "I don't buy drugs; they're available. I don't go looking for them." What is he protesting? "My whole life is a protest. There are so many people who would like me to be like the—dead."

Formerly, Robert demonstrated for Negro civil rights and against the war in Vietnam. He's thrown away his picket signs, symbols, he now thinks, of a "game" he played before LSD tuned him into larger realities and deeper insights. He's dropped out (protest is futile, he believes)— gone underground—and become part of the "love generation."[14]

To some, therefore, drugs may seem to offer solutions to major problems of life.

[14]*Ibid.*

Youth is an age of questioning, of learning for oneself what is real and true, a time of keen concern about "who am I?" For some youths, drugs offer new possibilities in this quest. They also offer an escape from an era of rapid, revolutionary change that leaves adults, as well as youths, bewildered and uneasy as to what tomorrow may bring. There are crucial struggles over civil rights and social injustice. The war in Vietnam is unpopular with many citizens, young and old. The cities show obvious decay; pollution of air, water, and land is increasing. Offstage is a menace of obliterating nuclear war.

Rapid social changes widen the "generation gap," states Dr. Kenneth Keniston, Yale psychologist, and the here-and-now becomes more important to the young who "can no longer commit themselves unquestionably to the life styles, attitudes, and skills of their parents. To do so is to condemn one's self to obsolesence in the modern world." Many youths live under tremendous pressure from their parents and others to excel in school, and, to some, "school work seems contrived, a form of marking time, and hence irrelevant," states Dr. Dana L. Farnsworth, Director of the University Health Services at Harvard.

Never before have so many of the nation's youth been so accustomed to affluence, with no worry about starvation, unemployment, or depression. Parents who have survived the Great Depression of the 1930s and have worked hard to give their children a better break, find their offsprings' rejection of hard-earned advantages difficult to understand. Further, they often react bitterly to young peoples' protests that the society they are growing up in is materialistic, commercialized, impersonal, automatic, full of social injustice, providing no opportunity for the individual and his inner feelings. Many adults feel that life has become just "too easy" for the youth of today, or that young people have "lost touch with reality."

Psychiatrists who have worked with many teen-agers and young adults have concluded that the youngsters often identify with a new notion that you can want experiences which are purely esthetic, purely on their own merits, even if they do not lead anywhere.

In general, the addict is a disordered person, undisciplined and insistent on the immediate satisfaction of his real or imagined needs. However, this general description is not very helpful, for it might also apply to many non-addicts. The fact is that recognition of the drug addict, especially when he is obtaining his customary dosage, is extremely difficult. The behavior of the drug addict is not well understood, and detection frequently requires the application of sophisticated laboratory techniques.

> Positive identification can only be made by laboratory examination. Even withdrawal symptoms, although highly suggestive, are in no sense specific, and therefore, are not conclusive.[15]

There are a few overt diagnostic characteristics, such as the scars and abscesses resulting from intravenous injections, and the pupil dilation and tremulousness caused by use of cocaine or Benzedrine. But it is difficult to recognize a marihuana smoker, although he sometimes has a characteristic facial flush. And opiate users can only be positively identified by urine analysis, which may detect traces of the drug as much as ten days after it was last used. Because of this difficulty in recognizing addicts, recognition should only be attempted under hospital conditions, that is, in a drug-free environment which permits prolonged observation and complete physical and laboratory examination.[16]

Although it is extremely difficult to recognize an addict on the basis of immediate physical evidence, as we have noted, there are other indications of addiction which eventually appear in his life style and behavior, and which can be observed over a period of time. The tolerant, large-dose, chronic drug abuser may not exhibit obvious physical signs of his drug usage, but he will show signs of social, economic, and emotional deterioration (e.g., downgrading of job or school work, rundown physical condition, and unkempt ap-

---

[15]A. J. Rogers, "Narcotic Addiction Among Young People," *Federal Probation*, 34, No. 2 (June 1970), 34–35.
[16]*Ibid.*, p. 35

A Special Problem: Drug Abuse—The Youthful Scene

pearance). (See Fig. 6–4.) Such a person also tends to become unreliable, irritable, and unstable. Various other behavioral changes are also quite predominant.

Some characteristics of the adolescent drug user are as follows:

1. He tends to be *materialistic* since, in a sense, he has ceased to believe that his emotional needs can be met in a positive manner.
2. He approaches life with a profound sense of *inadequacy* and *helplessness*, which overwhelms him and causes him to flee from the realities of everyday living. He seeks the comfortable vacuum that the drug offers him. The drug has value for the adolescent addict not solely because it can provide pleasurable sensations, but because it becomes a buffer between him and the society which he fears.
3. Since he is an escapist, he is *unable to relate* to other people in a meaningful, constructive, realistic fashion. He can only take from others in a dependent and passive manner and is unable to give anything in return in either a physical or an emotional sense.
4. He is usually involved in a *conflictual relationship with parental figures.* He feels that the parent does not understand him, and also anticipates that the parent will act in a manner that will be detrimental to his personal interests. On occasions, it is found that the parents of the drug addict are also inadequate people. They are unable to really live up to the criteria expected in a parent-child relationship. This weakness in the parental relationship permeates the entire living situation. Because of his relatively unstable, immature personality structure, the teen-age drug addict perceives his environmental situation out of perspective. As a result, he experiences great difficulty where only a moderate difficulty should exist.
5. *He perceives the adult world as an unstable place*, and he prefers to seek out the security of an infantile type of relationship. This infantile relationship may serve as a protection from dealing with the more complex situations and responsibilities that can be expected of one who aspires to be accepted as an adult.[17]

[17]For a readable discussion of the personality characteristics of a juvenile drug addict, refer to: E. Eldefonso, *Law Enforcement and the Youthful Offender: Juvenile Procedures* (New York: John Wiley, 1967), pp. 275–78.

Youthful World of Drugs

The Tragedy of Drugs

THIS YOUNG MAN, 20 YEARS OF AGE, WAS FOUND
DEAD IN A BOX CAR FROM AN OVERDOSE OF DRUGS.

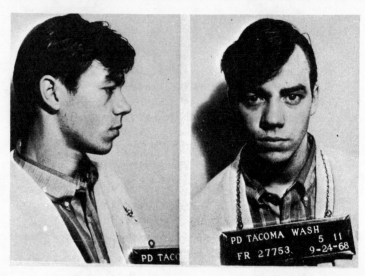

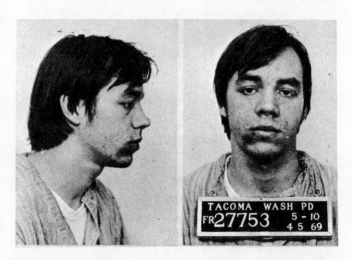

Fig. 6.4. (Reproduced with permission of the young man's father, in the hopes it may prevent others from becoming victims of similar tragedies)

A Special Problem: Drug Abuse—The Youthful Scene

A COPY OF THE NOTE LEFT BY HIM, AND FOUND IN
HIS SHIRT POCKET, HAS BEEN REPRODUCED BELOW.

Dear Father,
　　　I think you know the reason why I've done this its not easy to believe the real reason though. Dope ruined my life and took away my happyness forever I could never live in the state of mind I was in, so please don't hate me too much for what I have done I thought I found truth in what I was doing, experiencing life but. I found out too late that it was only death I was tripping on.
　　　Dad I hope I find happiness now knowing I destroyed my life and others with it. I hope to God ~~that~~ the people taking dope find what I found in it but only too soon. Goodby father and don't think you were ever cheated out of life because there is always time to learn to help. Your son Love Rick

Fig. 6.4.
(cont.)

Youthful World of Drugs

109

There is a significant difference between the adult abuser and the juvenile, or "teen-age" abuser. The juvenile presents a more complex picture than the adult. Going through adolescence is, under the best of circumstances, a difficult and complex process. Some authorities feel that boredom and lack of definite goals may contribute to juvenile troubles. One salient feature of adolescence is the need that all juveniles have to be accepted and "to belong." For many youths, a juvenile gang fills this need. By conforming to the gang's code of behavior, the juvenile gains recognition in his group. Often the degree of recognition he is given is in direct proportion to his willingness to defy legal, social, and parental authority. Juvenile drug abuse frequently stems from this "gang psychology." It usually begins in a gang or party setting. One member of the group starts, and the rest go along for fear of appearing "chicken."[18]

Varieties and Types of Drugs Abused

Wise police officers will try to lead from the strength of knowledge in discussing drugs with teen-agers. Only if they possess such knowledge are they likely to be effective and to speak intelligently.

Knowledge in this case must be based on the facts about the drugs themselves—what they are like and what they do to people. Table 6–1 provides a rundown of the principal drugs being used or abused by teen-agers and young adults.[19]

Stimulants

Amphetamines, first produced in the 1920s for medical use, stimulate the central nervous system and are best known for their effectiveness in combating fatigue and sleepiness.

[18]D. Wakefield, The Addict (New York: Fawcett Publications, 1963), p. 56.

[19]Excellent resources in this area are: G. McLean and H. Bowen's pamphlet, "Facts You Need to Know about Drug Abuse" (Palo Alto, Calif.: Darr Publishing Co., 1970), and the same authors' book, High on the Campus (Wheaton, Ill.: Tyndale House, 1970).

Table 6–1

The Major Mind-Affecting Drugs

		Slang Names	What They Are
ILLICIT (PROHIBITED) DRUGS*	HALLUCINOGENS	LSD, Acid	LSD-25 is a lysergic acid derivative. Mescaline is a chemical taken from peyote cactus. Psilocybin is synthesized from Mexican mushrooms.
	HEROIN	Snow, Stuff, H, Junk and others	Heroin is diacetylmorphine, an alkaloid derived from morphine; it does not occur in opium. A white, off-white, or brown crystalline powder, it has long been the drug of choice among opiate addicts. Its possession is illegal.
	MARIJUANA (Cannabis)	Joints, Sticks, Reefers, Weed, Grass, Pot, Muggles, Mooters, Indian hay, Loco-weed, Mu, Gigglesmoke, Griffo, Mohasky, Mary Jane	Marijuana is the dried flowering or fruiting top of the plant Cannabis Sativa L., commonly called Indian Hemp. Usually looks like fine, green tobacco. Its possession is illegal. Hashish is a preparation of cannabis, taken orally in many forms.
LEGITIMATE (PERMISSIVE) DRUGS†	AMPHETAMINE	Bennies, Co-pilots, Footballs, Hearts, Pep pills	Amphetamines are stimulants, prescribed by physicians chiefly to reduce appetite and to relieve minor cases of mental depression. Often used to promote wakefulness and/or increase energy.
	BARBITURATES	Red birds, Yellow jackets, Blue heavens, Goof balls	Barbiturates are sedatives, prescribed to induce sleep or, in smaller doses, to provide a calming effect. All are legally restricted to prescription use only. Dependence producing, both psychic and physical, with variable tolerance. Signs of physical dependence appear with doses well above therapeutic level.
	COCAINE	The Leaf, Snow, Speedballs (when mixed with heroin)	Extracted from the leaves of the coca bush. It is a white, odorless, fluffy powder that looks like crystalline snow.
	CODEINE	Schoolboy	A component of opium and a derivative of morphine, in most respects a tenth or less as effective as morphine, dose-wise.
	METHAMPHETAMINE	Speed, Crystal	Stimulant, closely related to amphetamine and ephedrine.
	MORPHINE	M, Dreamer, and many others	The principal active component of opium. Morphine sulphate: white crystalline powder, light porous cubes or small white tablets.

*Manufacture and distribution prohibited except for approved research purposes.
†Essential to the practice of medicine; legitimate manufacture and distribution are confined to ethical drugs.
Source: From American Social Health Association: "A Guide to Some Drugs Which Are Subject to Abuse."

Table 6-1 (cont.)

		How Taken	Primary Effect
ILLICIT (PROHIBITED) DRUGS*	HALLUCINOGENS	In tablet, capsule, ampul (hypodermic) form or in saturated sugar cubes.	All produce hallucinations, exhilaration, or depression, and can lead to serious mental changes, psychotic manifestations, suicidal or homicidal tendencies.
	HEROIN	May be taken by any route, usually by intravenous injection.	Like morphine in all respects, faster and shorter acting.
	MARIJUANA (Cannabis)	Marijuana smoked in pipes or cigarettes. Hashish is infrequently made into candy, sniffed in powder form, mixed with honey for drinking or with butter to spread on bread.	A feeling of great perceptiveness and pleasure can accompany even small doses. Erratic behavior, loss of memory, distortion of time and spatial perceptions, and hilarity without apparent cause occur. Marked unpredictability of effect.
LEGITIMATE (PERMISSIVE) DRUGS†	AMPHETAMINE	Orally as a tablet or capsule. Abusers may resort to intravenous injection.	Normal doses produce wakefulness, increased alertness and a feeling of increased initiative. Intravenous doses produce cocaine-like psychotoxic effects.
	BARBITURATES	Orally as a tablet or capsule. Sometimes intravenously by drug abusers.	Small amounts make the user relaxed, sociable, good-humored. Heavy doses make him sluggish, gloomy, sometimes quarrelsome. His speech is thick and he staggers. Sedation and incoordination progressive with dose, and at least additive with alcohol and/or other sedatives and tranquilizers.
	COCAINE	A surface active anesthetic; by abusers, taken orally or, most commonly intravenously alone, combined with or alternating with heroin. The coca leaves are chewed with lime, producing the effects of the contained cocaine.	Oral use is said to relieve hunger and fatigue, and produce some degree of exhilaration. Intravenous use produces marked psychotoxic effects, hallucinations with paranoid tendencies. Repetitive doses lead to maniacal excitation, muscular twitching, convulsive movements.
	CODEINE	Usually taken orally, in tablets, for pain; or in a liquid preparation, of variable alcohol content, for cough. Can be injected.	Analgesic and cough suppressant with very little sedation or exhilarant (euphoric) action. Dependence can be produced or partially supported, but large doses are required and risk is minor.
	METH-AMPHETAMINE	Orally, as tablets or in an elixir, or intravenously.	Effects resemble amphetamine but are more marked and toxicity greater.
	MORPHINE	May be taken by any route; its abusive use is mostly by intravenous injection.	Generally sedative and analgesic (rarely excitatory). The initial reaction is unpleasant to most people, but calming supersedes and, depending on dose, may progress to coma and death from respiratory failure.

Table 6–1 (cont.)

How to Spot Abuser	*Dangers*
Abusers may undergo complete personality changes, "see" smells, "hear" colors. They may try to fly or brush imaginary insects from their bodies, etc. Behavior is irrational. Marked depersonalization.	Very small quantities of LSD may cause hallucinations lasting for days or repetitive psychotoxic episodes, which may recur months after injection. Permanence of mental derangement is still a moot question. Damage to chromosomes, and hence potentially to offspring, has been demonstrated.
Morphine-like.	Like morphine; dependence usually develops more rapidly. Dependence liability is high.
Abusers may feel exhilarated or relaxed, stare off into space; be hilarious without apparent cause; have exaggerated sense of ability.	Because of the vivid visions and exhilaration which result from use of marijuana, abusers may lose all restraint and act in a manner dangerous to themselves and/or others. Accident prone because of time and space sense disturbance. Dependence (psychic but not physical) leads to anti-social behavior and could be forerunner of use of other drugs.
An almost abnormal cheerfulness and unusual increase in activity, jumpiness and irritability; hallucinations and paranoid tendencies after intravenous use.	Amphetamines can cause high blood pressure, abnormal heart rhythms and even heart attacks. Teenagers often take them to increase their "nerve." As a result, they may behave dangerously. Excess or prolonged usage can cause hallucinations, loss of weight, wakefulness, jumpiness and dangerous aggressiveness. Tolerance to large doses is acquired by abusers; psychic dependence develops but physical dependence does not; and there is no characteristic withdrawal syndrome.
The appearance of drunkenness with no odor of alcohol characterizes heavy dose. Sedation with variable ataxia.	Sedation, coma and death from respiratory failure. Inattentiveness may cause unintentional repetitious administration to a toxic level. Many deaths each year from intentional and unintentional overdose. Potentiation with alcohol particularly hazardous. The drug is addictive, causing physical as well as psychic dependency, and withdrawal phenomena are characteristically different from withdrawal of opiates.
Dilated pupils, hyperactive, exhilarated paranoic.	Convulsions and death may occur from overdose. Paranoic activity. Very strong psychic but no physical dependence and no tolerance.
Unless taken intravenously, very little evidence of general effect. Large doses are morphine-like.	Occasionally taken (liquid preparations) for kicks, but large amount required. Contribution of the alcohol content to the effect may be significant. Degree and risk of abuse very minor. Occasionally resorted to by opiate-dependent persons to tide them over with inadequate result.
Exteme restlessness and irritability; violence and paranoid reaction possible.	Excessive psychotoxic effects, sometimes with fatal outcome.
Constricted pupils. Calm, inattentive, "on the nod," with slow pulse and respiration.	Man is very sensitive to the respiratory depressant effect until tolerance develops. Psychic and physical dependence and tolerance develop readily, with a characteristic withdrawal syndrome.

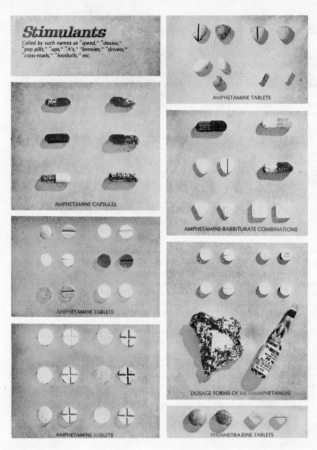

Fig. 6.5.

They are also sometimes used to curb appetite in medically supervised weight-reduction programs. The most commonly used stimulants are Benzedrine, Dexedrine, and Methedrine. (See Figure 6–5.)

Slang terms for these drugs include pep pills, bennies, and speed.

Examples: Benzedrine (bennies), Methedrine (crystal), Dexedrine (dexies, Xmas trees), and cocaine (coke, snow).

Abuse: Because the body develops a tolerance to amphetamines, abusers increase their dosages gradually, a practice which exaggerates the normal effects of these drugs and results in:

A Special Problem: Drug Abuse—The Youthful Scene

Euphoria	Restlessness
Excitability	Enlarged pupils
Alertness	Sleeplessness
Tremor of the hands	Heavy perspiration
Reduction of awareness of fatigue	Loss of appetite
Talkativeness	Weight loss

Stimulant drugs increase the heart rate, raise the blood pressure, dilate the pupils, and cause palpitations (throbbing heart and rapid breathing), dry mouth, sweating, headache, diarrhea, and paleness. They also depress the appetite.

Are These Stimulants Addicting? Benzedrine, Dexedrine and other stimulant drugs do not produce physical dependence as do the "hard" drugs (drugs made from opium; i.e., morphine, paregoric, codeine, etc.) or narcotics. The body does not become physically dependent on their continued use. It does, however, develop a tolerance to these drugs, and increasingly larger doses are required to feel their effects.

There is another kind of dependence medical authorities identify with the abuse of stimulants, called "psychological dependence." Abuse can become a habit for mental or emotional reasons, with the person "getting used to" turning to the drug for its effects.

Depressants

Barbiturates—Sedatives, Sleeping Pills: The barbiturates are a large family of drugs derived from barbituric acid, which was developed in Germany in the nineteenth century. Since then, innumerable barbiturates have been synthesized and prepared for medical use under trade names such as Seconal, Phenobarbital, and Nembutal. These drugs are available in liquids, tablets, capsules, and various other forms (Figure 6–6).

Identification of Barbiturates: Barbiturates are known to drug abusers as barbs, candy, goof balls, sleeping pills, or peanuts. Specific types are often named after their color or shape. For example, solid yellow capsules are known to abusers as yellows, yellow jackets, or nimbies. Red capsules are called reds, pinks, red birds, red devils, seggy, and seccy.

Varieties and Types of Drugs Abused

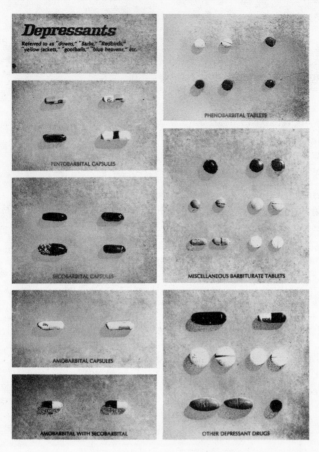

Depressants

Referred to as "downs," "Barbs," "Redbirds," "yellow jackets," "goofballs," "blue heavens," etc.

PENTOBARBITAL CAPSULES

SECOBARBITAL CAPSULES

AMOBARBITAL CAPSULES

AMOBARBITAL WITH SECOBARBITAL

PHENOBARBITAL TABLETS

MISCELLANEOUS BARBITURATE TABLETS

OTHER DEPRESSANT DRUGS

Fig. 6.6.

Red and blue capsules are known as rainbows, reds and blues, or double trouble. Solid blue capsules are known by abusers as blues, blue birds, blue devils, or blue heavens.

Examples: Seconal (red devils), Nembutal (yellow jackets), and Phenobarbital (phennies).

Abuse: Continued and excessive dosages of barbiturates result in:

Euphoria	Loss of balance and falling
Impaired judgment	Quick temper
Retarded reaction time	Quarrelsome disposition
Slurring speech	Coma (with danger of
Staggering	pneumonia and death)
	Sleep induction

Authorities consider the barbiturates highly dangerous when taken without medical advice and prescription. Because these drugs are commonly prescribed by doctors, many people mistakenly consider them safe to use freely and as they choose. They are not. Overdose can cause death.

Barbiturates distort the way in which people see things and slow down their reactions and responses. They are an important cause of automobile accidents, especially when taken together with alcohol. Barbiturates tend to heighten the effects of alcohol.

Users may react to the drug more strongly at one time than at another. They may become confused about how many pills they have taken, and die of an accidental overdose. Barbiturates are a leading cause of accidental poison deaths in the United States. Because they are easily obtained and produce sleep readily, barbiturates are also one of the main methods people choose to commit suicide.

These drugs are *physically addicting*. The body becomes dependent upon them and needs increasingly higher doses to feel their effects. Some experts consider barbiturate addiction more difficult to cure than narcotic dependency. If the drug is withdrawn abruptly, the user suffers withdrawal sickness accompanied by cramps, nausea, delirium, convulsions, and, in some cases, sudden death. Therefore, withdrawal should take place in a hospital over a period of several weeks on gradually reduced dosages. It takes several months for the body to return to normal.

What Are the Legal Controls?   Stimulants and barbiturates are regulated by the Bureau of Narcotics and Dangerous Drugs, a division of the Department of Justice. Laws provide for a strict accounting of supplies of these drugs by the manufacturer, distributor, and seller and restrict the user to five refills of the prescription, at the discretion of his physician. The drugs can be had legally only through a doctor. Illicit manufacturing and dispensing of barbiturates can bring fines up to $10,000 and prison sentences up to 5 years. Those convicted of selling the drugs to persons under 21 can be fined $15,000 to $20,000 and receive 10 to 15 years in jail. Merely possessing these drugs illegally can bring a fine of from $1,000 to $10,000 and/or imprisonment of 1 to 3 years. State laws also control their illicit use.

Varieties and Types of Drugs Abused

Plastic glues vary in chemical composition, depending on the specific formula used by the manufacturer, but all of these cements contain highly volatile organic solvents—substances considered in industry to be safe when inhaled in low vapor concentration, but known to be dangerously toxic when inhaled in high concentration. Solvene is a prime constitutent of most glues and of plastic cements.

The effects of glue sniffing are comparable, except in degree, to the effects of a general anesthetic upon the body. The glue sniffer experiences a tingling sensation in his head —a lightness and an exhilaration known to him as a "jag." If he continues to inhale the glue, he will experience a state similar to alcoholic intoxication.

Identification of Dangerous Glue: Quick-drying plastic cement, frequently called airplane glue, as well as certain solvents such as benzene, carbon tetrachloride, and ethyl alcohol, can be very harmful when breathed.

Abuse: Inhalation of such toxic fluids commonly result in:

Euphoria	Staggering
Intoxication	Irritability
Dizziness	Rash, foolish, and even
Possible loss of consciousness	dangerous actions
Slurred speech	

The "glue-sniffer" commonly:

Has inflamed eyes
Has irritated nose and lung tissue
Loses appetite and weight
Feels constantly sick

*LSD-25 D-Lysergic Acid
Diethylamide Tartrate
(A Hallucinogenic Drug)*

Identification of LSD-25:   LSD-25 is an odorless, tasteless, and colorless chemical which, when taken in even the smallest quantities, is likely to cause the mind to react in strange, unpredictable, and uncontrollable ways.

People who use LSD say that it has a number of psychological effects. The first effects, they indicate, are likely to be sudden changes in their physical senses. Walls may appear to move, and colors seem stronger and more brilliant. Users are likely to "see" unusual patterns unfolding before them. Flat objects seem to stand out in three dimensions. Taste, smell, hearing, and touch seem more acute. One sensory impression may be translated or merged into another; for example, music may appear as a color, and colors may seem to have different tastes (Figure 6–7).

One of the most confusing yet common reactions among users is the feeling of two strong and opposite emotions at the same time—they can feel both happy and sad at once, or

Fig. 6.7.

Varieties and Types of Drugs Abused

depressed and elated, or relaxed and tense. Arms and legs may feel both heavy and light.

Users also report a sensation of losing the normal feeling of boundaries between body and space. This sometimes gives them the notion that they can fly or float with ease.

Effects can be different at different times in the same individual. Researchers have found, even in carefully controlled studies, that responses to the drug cannot be predicted. For this reason, users refer to "good trips" or "bad trips" to describe their experience.

As to the *physical* effects, an average dose of LSD, amounting to a speck, has an effect that lasts for about eight to ten hours. Users take it in a sugar cube, a cracker, or a cookie, or they lick it off a stamp or other object impregnated with the drug. It increases the pulse and causes a rise in blood pressure and temperature, dilated eye pupils, shaking of the hands and feet, cold, sweaty palms, a flushed or pale face, shivering, and chills with goose pimples.

Is LSD Dangerous? Recent reports from hospitals in areas where LSD is used without close medical supervision warn of definite dangers. These include:

1. PANIC. The user may grow frightened because he cannot stop the drug's action, and he may fear that he is losing his mind.
2. PARANOIA. He may become increasingly suspicious, feeling that someone is trying to harm him or control his thinking. This feeling generally lasts 72 hours after the drug has warn off.
3. RECURRENCE. Days, weeks, or even months after the individual has stopped using LSD, the things he saw and felt while on the drug may recur and make him fear he is going insane.
4. ACCIDENTAL DEATH. Because the LSD user may feel that he can fly or float, he may try to leap out of a high window or from other heights and fall to his death. Or, he may drive or walk in front of a moving car because he thinks he cannot be harmed. Such accidents have been reported.

How Does the Law View LSD? Because LSD is a dangerous drug when not used for research under medical supervision, it is closely regulated by the Bureau of Narcotics and Dangerous Drugs. The law provides strict penalties for anyone who illegally produces, sells or disposes of dangerous drugs like LSD. Conviction can bring a fine of $1,000 to $10,000 and/or imprisonment for up to 5 years. For persons over 18 years of age who sell or give drugs to anyone under 21, the law provides penalties of 10 to 15 years in jail and fines up to $20,000.

Marihuana

Marihuana is a drug found in the flowering tops and leaves of the Indian hemp plant, *Cannabis sativa*. The plant grows in mild climates in countries around the world, especially in Mexico, Africa, India, and the Middle East. It also grows in the United States, where the drug is known as pot, tea, grass, weed, Mary Jane, and by other names (Figures 6–8a and 6–8b).

Fig. 6.8a
Marihuana plant. Courtesy of Sgt. James J. Guido, Director, Police Athletic League, San Jose Police Department, San Jose, California.

Varieties and Types of Drugs Abused

HOW TO RECOGNIZE MARIJUANA

Courtesy of the Ambassador College Research Department.

Fig. 6.8b. Marihuana in various forms as displayed by an agent of the Los Angeles Police Narcotics Division. Torn package shows raw marihuana as it is shipped in *brick form*. *Small vial* in lower right holds marihuana *seeds*. Also, marihuana *cookie* is shown. Note how marihuana cigarettes can be distinguished quite easily from ordinary commercial cigarettes, contrary to popular misconception.

A Special Problem: Drug Abuse—The Youthful Scene

For use as a drug, the leaves and flowers of the plant are dried and crushed or chopped into small pieces. This green product is usually rolled and smoked in short cigarettes or in pipes, or it can be taken in food. The cigarettes are commonly known as reefers, joints, and sticks. The smoke from marihuana is harsh, and smells like burnt rope or dried grasses. Its sweetish odor is easily recognized.

The strength of the drug differs from place to place, depending on where and how it is grown, how it is prepared for use, and how it is stored. The marihuana grown in the United States is much weaker than the kind grown in Asia, Africa, or the Near East.

When smoked, marihuana quickly enters the bloodstream and acts on the brain and nervous system. It affects the user's mood and thinking. Its pathway into the brain is not yet understood. Some scientists report that the drug accumulates in the liver. Because it may cause hallucinations when taken in very large doses, it is classed as a mild "hallucinogen." Just how the drug works in the body and how it produces its effects have not yet been discovered by medical science.

The long-term physical effects of taking marihuana are not yet known. The kind of research needed to learn the results of chronic use has not yet been done.

The more obvious physical reactions include rapid heart beat, lowering of body temperature, and sometimes reddening of the eyes. The drug also changes blood sugar levels, stimulates the appetite, and dehydrates the body. Users may get talkative, loud, unsteady, or drowsy, and find it hard to coordinate their movements.

The drug's effects on the emotions and senses vary widely, depending on the amount and strength of the marihuana used. The social setting in which it is taken and what the user expects also influence his reaction to the drug.

Usually, when it is smoked, marihuana's effect is felt quickly, in about 15 minutes. Its effects can last from two to four hours. The range of effects can vary from depression to a feeling of excitement. Some users, however, experience no change of mood at all. Many users experience distorted senses of time and of distance. A minute may seem like an hour. Something near may seem far away.

Varieties and Types of Drugs Abused

Dependence: Marihuana may develop a psychological dependence in the user. Because so many users of narcotics report previous use of marihuana, concern should be given not only to the habit-forming use of marihuana, but also to the serious possibility that it will serve as a stepping-stone to more serious drug addition.

What Are the Laws Dealing with Marihuana? Under federal law, to have, give, or sell marihuana in the United States is a felony, which is a serious crime. Federal and many state laws deal with the drug as severely as if it were a narcotic.

The federal penalty for possession of marihuana is 2 to 10 years imprisonment for the first offense, 5 to 20 years for the second offense, and 10 to 40 years for further offenses. Fines of up to $20,000 for the first or subsequent offenses may be imposed. State laws also control the illicit use of these drugs. For transfer or sale of the drug, the first offense may bring a 5 to 20 year sentence and a fine of up to $20,000; two or more offenses, 10 to 40 years in prison. If a person over 19 sells to a minor under 18 years of age, he is subject to a fine of up to $20,000 and/or 10 to 40 years in prison for the first offense, with no suspension of sentence, probation, or parole.

What Are the Special Risks for Young Users? Breaking the laws dealing with marihuana can have serious effects on the lives of young people. They may find their education interrupted and their future shadowed or altered by having a police record. An arrest or conviction for a felony (in some states possession is a misdemeanor and selling a felony) can complicate their life and plans at many turns. For example, in many states, a person with a police record must meet special conditions to obtain or renew a driver's license. Conviction can prevent a person from being able to enter a profession such as medicine, law, or teaching. It can make it difficult for him to get a responsible position in business or industry. Special hearings are necessary before he can hold a government job. Before a student tries marihuana, he should be aware of the social and legal facts about getting involved with the drug.

Other risks are pointed out by experts on human growth and development. They say that a more subtle result of drug abuse on the young person is its effect on his personality growth and development.

Narcotics

The term narcotic refers, generally, to opium and pain-relieving drugs made from opium, such as heroin, morphine, paregoric, and codeine. These and other opiates are obtained from the juice of the poppy seed. Several synthetic drugs, such as Demerol, and Dolophine, are also classed as narcotics. Opiates are widely used in medicine as pain relievers. Cocaine, made from coca leaves, and marihuana are classified legally but not chemically as narcotic drugs.

Since heroin appears to be the narcotic used by most addicts today, the following questions and answers deal mainly with heroin.

What Is Narcotic Addiction? When the abuser of a narcotic gets "hooked"—meaning addicted—his body requires repeated and larger doses of the drug. Once the habit starts, larger and larger doses are required to get the same effects. This happens because the body develops a "tolerance" for the drug.

One of the signs of heroin addiction is withdrawal sickness. When the addict stops using the drug, he may sweat, shake, or get chills, experience nausea and diarrhea, and suffer sharp abdominal and leg cramps. Modern treatments help the addict through these withdrawal stages. Science now has new evidence that the body's physical addiction may last much longer than previously believed.

Psychological dependence is also connected with the use of narcotics. That is, taking the drug also becomes a habit for emotional reasons. For example, the addict may come to depend on the drug as a way to escape facing life.

Narcotic use can become even more of an escape than expected, because large or unexpectedly pure doses can and not uncommonly do result in death.

What Is the Effect of the Drug? Typically, the first emotional reaction to heroin is reduction of tension, easing of fears, and relief from worry. Feeling "high" may be followed by a period of inactivity bordering on stupor.

Varieties and Types of Drugs Abused

Heroin, which is usually mixed into a liquid solution and injected into a vein, appears to dull the edges of reality. Addicts have reported that heroin "makes my troubles roll off my mind" and "makes me feel more sure of myself."

The drug depresses certain areas of the brain, and may reduce hunger, thirst, and the sex drive. Because addicts do not usually feel hungry, their hospital care may include treatment for malnutrition. The drug may also reduce feelings of pain.

Withdrawal symptoms appear in the addicted person about 18 hours after the drug has been discontinued.

In general, effects of the drug are influenced by many factors. These include the user's personality, size and frequency of dose, and how the drug is taken.

Does Addiction Lead to Crime? Some studies suggest that many known narcotic addicts have had some trouble with the law before they became addicted. Once addicted, they may become even more involved with crime because it costs so much to support the heroin habit. An addict may have to spend up to $75 to $100 to buy his day's supply of heroin.

Most authorities agree that the addict's involvement with crime is not a direct effect of the drug itself, but that crime is usually the only means he has of obtaining the money he needs to support his habit. His crimes are nearly always thefts or other crimes against property, and not often crimes of passion or violence.

What Are the Legal Penalties? Federal penalties for illegal narcotics usage were established under the Harrison Act of 1914, which provides that illegal possession of narcotics is punishable by fines and/or imprisonment. Sentences can range from 2 to 10 years for the first offense, 5 to 20 years for the second, and 10 to 20 years for further offenses.

Illegal sale of narcotics can mean a fine of $20,000 and a sentence of 5 to 20 years for the first offense, and 10 to 40 years for further offenses. A person who sells narcotics to someone under 18 is refused parole and probation even for the first offense. If the drug is heroin, he can be sentenced to life imprisonment or to death.

The Harrison Act has been used as a model for most state laws, and it has been the practice among both federal and state judges to impose severe sentences for narcotics violations.

A Special Problem: Drug Abuse—The Youthful Scene

Summary

Drug abuse is probably as old as the earliest civilizations. The hemp plant, *Cannabis sativa*, was described as a source of long textile fibers as early as 1200 B.C., and its narcotic properties were documented in Chinese writings by 200 A.D. Marihuana has thus been used for centuries for its intoxicant and euphoric properties. Some of the other drugs being abused today are relatively new, for example, LSD. Chapter 6 presents a historical discussion of the problem of drugs, which is carried through to contemporary times.

Currently, there are an estimated 25,000 addicts in New York City alone, and an increasing percentage of our youth population is utilizing drugs. Although marihuana remains the favorite student drug, students also use Mescaline (a form of peyote), speed (usually Methedrine), and LSD. This chapter points out the extent of the drug problem in today's youth culture, introducing data from reliable sources.

Information pertaining to the "Youthful World of Drugs" indicates that the problem of drug abuse knows no boundaries. While most of the serious drug problems in our society are in inner cities, abuse is also widespread in more affluent suburban areas.

The reasons for drug abuse are explored as well as the appeals drugs offer. The question of "why drugs?" is analyzed. It is pointed out that the drug abuser, due to an inadequate personality, fails to identify with mature, adult goals. He therefore finds drugs necessary in blocking inhibitions and responsibilities and in creating a pleasure-seeking environment in which he can pursue pleasurable activities. From this analysis evolves a "Portrait of an Adolescent Drug Abuser."

The chapter concludes with a review of the various types of drugs abused, including information concerning their identification, the physical and psychological reaction they trigger, the extent of addiction caused, if any, and the legal restrictions on their possession and use.

Selected References

AUSUBEL, D. P., *Drug Addiction: Physiological, Psychological, and Sociological Aspects*, Chap. 7. New York: Random House, Inc., 1958.

Bureau of Narcotics, U. S. Treasury Department, *Traffic in Opium and Other Dangerous Drugs*. Washington, D.C.: Government Printing Office, Annual Statistical Report.

BLUM, R., and J. WAHL, "Police Views and Drug Abuse," *Utopiates*, entire study. New York: Atherton, 1970.

Drug Abuse: Game Without Winners. Washington, D. C.: Government Printing Office, 1965 (pamphlet).

McLEAN, G., and H. BOWEN, *High on the Campus*, Chaps. 1–3. Wheaton, Ill.: Tyndale House, 1970.

New Facts About Marijuana. Pasadena, Calif.: Ambassador College Research Department, 1970 (pamphlet).

SKOLNICK, J. H., *Justice without a Trial: Law Enforcement in a Democratic Society*, Chaps. 1–6. New York: John Wiley & Sons, Inc., 1966.

Task Force Report: Narcotics and Drug Abuse, The President's Commission on Law Enforcement and Administration of Justice. Washington, D. C.: Government Printing Office, 1967.